PENGUIN BOOKS

Why We Read

Why We Read

Seventy Writers on Non-Fiction

Edited by Josephine Greywoode

PENGUIN BOOKS

PENGUIN BOOKS

UK | USA | Canada | Ireland | Australia
India | New Zealand | South Africa

Penguin Books is part of the Penguin Random House group of companies
whose addresses can be found at global.penguinrandomhouse.com

First published 2022
003

Set in 9.5/13pt Sabon LT Std
Typeset by Jouve (UK), Milton Keynes
Printed and bound in Great Britain by Clays Ltd, Elcograf S.p.A.

The authorized representative in the EEA is Penguin Random House Ireland,
Morrison Chambers, 32 Nassau Street, Dublin D02 YH68

A CIP catalogue record for this book is available from the British Library

ISBN: 978-1-802-06095-9

www.greenpenguin.co.uk

Penguin Random House is committed to a
sustainable future for our business, our readers
and our planet. This book is made from Forest
Stewardship Council® certified paper.

Contents

Anthony Aguirre   1

Hilton Als   3

Abhijit Banerjee   4

Simon Baron-Cohen   5

Alison Bashford   7

Milo Beckman   9

Erica Benner   12

Ananyo Bhattacharya   14

James Bridle   16

Clare Carlisle   18

Shami Chakrabarti   20

Clare Chambers   22

Ha-Joon Chang   24

Paul Collier   25

Paul Davies   26

Richard Dawkins   29

Christopher de Hamel   33

Matthew Desmond   35

Jared Diamond   37

Dennis Duncan   40

George Dyson   43

David Edgerton   44

Jordan Ellenberg   47

Richard J. Evans   49

Seb Falk   52

Niall Ferguson   55

Nicci Gerrard   58

Gerd Gigerenzer   60

Malcolm Gladwell   63

John Gray   66

Jonathan Haidt   68

Thomas Halliday   70

Sudhir Hazareesingh   72

Peter Hennessy   75

Scott Hershovitz   76

Rosemary Hill   79

Clare Jackson   81

Jennifer Jacquet   83

Lucy Jones   85

Marit Kapla   87

Alex Kerr   89

Ian Kershaw   92

Emma Jane Kirby   94

Ivan Krastev   97

Michael Lewis   98

Daniel Lieberman   100

Kate Manne   102

Catherine Merridale   103

Rana Mitter   105

George Monbiot   106

Timothy Morton   107

Jan-Werner Müller   111

Veronica O'Keane   113

Helen Parr   116

Jordan Peterson   117

Steven Pinker   120

CONTENTS

Serhii Plokhy   122

Carlo Rovelli   123

Priya Satia   124

John Sellars   130

Emma Smith   132

Daniel Susskind   134

Sofi Thanhauser   136

Shashi Tharoor   138

Gaia Vince   140

Esmé Weijun Wang   143

Ralf Webb   145

David Wengrow   147

Lea Ypi   150

Slavoj Žižek   153

Anthony Aguirre

author of *Cosmological Koans*

If we imagine a library of *all possible books*, like Borges' fabled Library of Babel, it feels at first like overwhelming plenitude: so much information! But a bit more thought leads to a profound disappointment: in fact, such a library contains no information at all.

In his world-shaping article 'A Mathematical Theory of Communication' (1948), Claude Shannon pointed to exactly why this is. A random sequence of characters contains zero information; information lies in the choosing of one sequence among all of the possibilities. Just so, Borges' library contains books, but only contains *information* if someone identifies some of the books as interesting. The information is precisely the pointing to.

We can follow this intuition further. In some pieces of text, you can imagine swapping out words or whole sentences and barely changing the overall meaning. In others, as carefully crafted as a mathematical equation, every symbol sits carefully in its place. Shannon instructs us here too: we are sensing, in this deliberation, the presence of real information.

Today, we're trying our hardest to build an internet – or even a world – of Babel. We imagine that more bits are better. More text, from more people. Images adorning text, when they add nothing, because they catch the eye; video because it attracts more viewers, who 'engage more'; dozens of news stories conveying one fact (or worse, none); academic careers judged by sheer number of papers; machine-learning language models with the facsimile of intelligence churning out almost-believable prose. We have many more bits than anyone could ever want.

We need more pointing – an information ecosystem that rewards careful selection, not quantity, of bits. One that recognizes that some well-crafted sentences about the right things are worth finding, and elevating, and pointing to. Maybe we'll have that someday. In the meantime, we can activate that system in ourselves. The books surviving today from hundreds of years of writers have been selected by history and society. The books recommended by a trusted friend or well-curated list are special. Sentences and pages edited in a real process, paid for by their authors with years of their life to culminate in one work – these are a treasure. They are why we read.

Hilton Als
author of *White Girls*

Reading is writing's dearest companion. But I didn't become a serious reader until I was ten, by which time I had been writing for two years. That is, I became a writer – *knew* I was a writer – before I read many books. Writing, for me, was a way of expressing my private thoughts; I grew up in a large family where, it seems, everyone talked all the time. Writing was a way of getting a word in. My word. My mother and older sister were readers, so, it was inevitable that books would catch up with me, or I with them; and when I did, my world grew in ways I couldn't have imagined without them. I still feel the same way.

Abhijit Banerjee
co-author of *Good Economics for Hard Times*

Every author carefully sets up a game for us. I read to step inside the game and play: to spot the rhythms, the very special way the consonants knock into each other, to hear the echoes, internal and external, make connections and guess the ones the author wanted us to find. To follow the threads to where the author wants us to go, but to spot the red herrings before we get enmeshed with them; to listen to the music and lightness of the early words and try to guess how it will bring us to the darkness that is presaged by the title or a blurb. To spot where the rabbit gets put in the hat, where the moral dilemma starts to unfold, the exact point where there is the tiniest hint of the unlikely love that will eventually bloom. To cry when the weight becomes exactingly heavy, to smile when a play of words catches us by surprise, to laugh out loud when the anticipated contretemps ultimately arrives. Not all books manage to get me there, in part no doubt because I missed something critical, but I go into every book expecting some play. And even if the surprise does not arrive, even if the beautiful beginning descends into a shrill middle and a lame ending, even if the *Deus* has to emerge from the *machina* to help the story resolve itself, there is pleasure in wondering how it could have been different. I am a willing reader of all books as long as they come with an invitation to play and a twinkle in the author's eye.

Simon Baron-Cohen
author of *The Pattern Seekers*

Four thousand years ago, the earliest fictional story was written: the *Epic of Gilgamesh*. Its twelve chapters were written on a clay tablet.

In this story, Gilgamesh, a tyrannical king, meets Enkidu, a wild man who lives with the animals. The two men fight, Gilgamesh wins, yet the two of them become friends. Together they go on an adventure in the Cedar Forest and slay monsters, but tragically Enkidu dies. Gilgamesh, suffering the pain of grief, embarks on a quest to escape death by achieving godly immortality.

Clearly, back 4,000 years ago and still today, we readers love to hear an author tell a good story about a character's thoughts and feelings. We read because we want to broaden our own experience of the world, to find out about someone else's experience, thoughts and feelings – the writer's. In short, we want to enter the mind of the author. And the author writes a book to communicate their thoughts and feelings to their readers. In short, the author wants to enter the mind of the reader.

So one reason we read is that we – both writer and reader – empathize. We just can't help it.

But another reason we read is that we – both writer and reader – systemize. A book is simply a *system* or set of rules, in this case for how particular marks (etched in a clay tablet or written on paper) refer to a particular object or idea. Humans have been inventing different systems to get ideas and information from an author's mind into a reader's mind. Today, we can think of books that are digital or bound, printed or audible. And the production of books at scale was only made possible by the invention of the printing press in 1440. Before that, for 2,000 years, books were hand-printed or copied by hand. And going back to 4,000 years ago, books took the form of scrolls and sheets of papyrus, and, 5,000 years ago, clay tablets.

Even earlier, the precursors of the book were other systems of communication, such as cave paintings that are 40,000 years old or engravings that are 75,000 years old. These changing formats all speak to the human capacity for the invention of *systems*. Humans systemize – again, we just can't help it.

There are many other reasons for why we read. For example, we find pleasure in imagining a fictional reality, in being transported into another world, in learning from a writer by downloading their knowledge, in learning information about the world that is outside our first-hand experience, in discovering and organizing facts, in sitting with a child to entertain them with stories, or in playing with language itself.

But all of these other reasons ultimately boil down to our uniquely human abilities: to empathize or systemize.

Alison Bashford

author of *An Intimate History of Evolution*

TRAVELLING THROUGH NON-FICTION

I read non-fiction in exchange for a historian's salary, a secret that in the telling might shatter my luck. It's my job to read the same books that my historical subjects did, taking me to the foreign country that is our past, their present. Often enough, it's an unlikely pleasure. This summer, I'm reading books from the library of the classical political economist Thomas Robert Malthus. Given his dour reputation this might seem to warrant payment. But no: it's a delight. He would certainly have a view on the 'value' in my secret exchange of reading-for-money, since of course I'd also read it all for nothing.

His own books are sequestered behind heavy oak doors at the back of the Old Library of Jesus College, Cambridge: a modest gentleman's library *circa* 1800, all within an arm's reach. Adam Smith is first up. Malthus spent his entire adult life teaching fifteen-year-old man-boys at the East India Company College how to read and understand *The Wealth of Nations*. I can scribble happily away in my Penguin Classics edition, even as I carefully turn the pages of Malthus's 1776 copy. Marginalia upon marginalia. As a researcher, reading and writing is often one act.

For every economic treatise in this library there is a fiction title, and, perhaps surprisingly, far more Regency plays than novels or Romantic poetry. A lover of the theatre, the apparently stern but in fact much-liked Malthus purchased printed editions of the plays he routinely enjoyed at Covent Garden. James Boaden's '*Fontainville Forest*, a play in 5 acts', for example, founded on the *Romance of the Forest* by the gothic novelist of the 1790s Ann Radcliffe. Comedies too, like Richard Cumberland's *The Fashionable Lover*: 'Act

1, Scene 1: A hall in Lord Abberville's house, with a stair-case seen through an arch. Several domestics waiting in rich liveries. Flourish of French-horns.' Who wouldn't want to be transported to the Theatre Royal, Drury Lane? But do we still want to *read* such things? Probably not. That era has long gone.

Looking over Malthus's shelves, I suddenly see a non-fiction genre that has stuck like bookbinder's glue: travel writing. His library is overflowing with voyage and travel and expedition accounts. That reading experience is effortlessly shared between his century and ours, as familiar and popular as play scripts have become foreign and strange. Malthus sat in his chair and read Henry Bradshaw Fearon's *Sketches of America: A Narrative of a Journey of Five Thousand Miles Through the Eastern and Western States of America* (1818), much as I read Paul Theroux's *Deep South: Four Seasons on Back Roads* (2016). Malthus read Henry Fielding's *Journal of a Voyage to Lisbon* (1755) and Henry Swinburne's *Travels in the Two Sicilies* (1790), just as I read Jordan Salama's *Every Day the River Changes: Four Weeks Down the Magdalena* (2021) and Jonathan Raban's *Coasting: A Private Voyage* (2003). Malthus even read James Cook, *Voyage Towards the South Pole, and Round the World* (1777), while I read Mark Adams's *Meet me in Atlantis: Across Three Continents in Search of the Legendary Sunken City* (2016).

The conventions and pleasures and indulgence of travel writing have barely changed: first person; past tense; cross-cultural; observational and inspirational; informative and sensory. Voyages and journeys, discovery and rediscovery without moving anything except our page-turning hands.

Milo Beckman

author of *Math Without Numbers*

When I was a child I found a home in non-fiction reading. Thirsty to learn whatever I could about the world, I read science, biography, world history and politics. From my bedroom I felt that I could travel the globe and see from the eyes of people who had died long before I was born. For whatever reason, fiction didn't captivate me in the same way – it felt untrustworthy. (Macbeth did *what*? No, he didn't.) But non-fiction allowed me to live several decades of vicarious experience in a matter of weeks. It tied together ideas I'd always seen as separate, giving me new lenses with which to view the world around me. When I did look up from the books, I'd experience my actual life as if I were a traveller in my own hometown.

I especially want to give a shoutout to the sometimes overlooked genre of abstract, non-narrative non-fiction. Yes, it may not be for everyone, but I absolutely love to sit down with a dense academic tome and just pore. Talk about escape! If you think Narnia is a distant reality, try homotopy groups! I don't care if it's on morphology or fluid mechanics; I can lose hours to a good text. Reading and rereading, underlining and highlighting and translating as best I can out of the particular jargon spoken by this subculture of specialists. There's an element of sport to it: can I break into this abstruse crypt of a book and hold its rare knowledge in my hands? Or will it slip away? It's a great way to completely detach from the world around me.

There's also a certain beauty to this sort of information-dense non-fiction, in my view. It may not have the traditional aesthetic markings of a great book, but Theda Skocpol's *States and Social Revolutions* is one of the more surprising and rewarding books I've had the pleasure to engage with. While reading this book, on and off for nine months, I felt I was running my fingers blindly through a thousand twisted threads, loosely tied together, presented to me in situ. I was not being taken for a ride, persuaded, or even really instructed. This book existed simply to preserve a wealth of knowledge for future safe-keeping. I as the reader was participating in that act of preservation, by taking this trove into my head, incorporating it into my under-standing of the world, and translating it into my everyday conversations.

If you really want to get grandiose about it, you could say that the special power of humanity lies in this ability to maintain useful information across generations. Our oral traditions and especially our written traditions give to our systems of knowledge a life beyond the normal limit of mortality. Through books, our memories can outlast the capacity of any one mind to hold them. There's a reason thriving societies have great libraries, why rulers throughout history have depended on the counsel of literate scholars, and why invading empires ban and burn books. Reading and writing, learn-ing and teaching, are the legs of the relay race of culture. When I participate in these activities, particularly with important and hard-won knowledge, I feel that I've carried the torch.

That's why it's essential to be thoughtful about which knowledge we preserve and pass on. The power of the non-fiction pen is so immense that, for nearly all of modern history, as well as in many traditional societies, it's been withheld as an exclusive tool of ruling elites. What better way for the powerful to shape the course of his-tory than by maintaining the exclusive right to control the public's understanding of it? Today, even as new platforms of influence dis-empower the old gatekeepers, we see this pattern of social control continuing. We see authoritarians tightening their grips over offline and online content, perennial struggles over textbooks and curricula escalating to new heights, all while well-funded campaigns of legit-imization and delegitimization battle to sway our attention and trust. As the fire of literacy burns ever brighter, the question of *who* and *what* to read becomes more open-ended, more difficult, and more important.

When I started keeping a book log, somewhere around age 15, I quickly noticed that I was almost exclusively reading books by white men with academic backgrounds, from the US or UK. I was so embarrassed! Here I was, considering myself a well-rounded scholar, while hardly reading beyond my own intellectual backyard! So I started making a conscious effort to seek out authors from different professional, cultural, gender, class, and language backgrounds. It's no exaggeration to say that this one decision shaped my life and my thinking more than any other.

I felt some friction at first, as I dived into books with themes and settings entirely foreign to me. 'Why am I reading this?' I'd think. 'This isn't me.' There was plenty of discomfort and shame, too, as I was forced to see myself and my culture described from the outside – not always with the highest regard. But I stuck with the plan, reading not as a critic but as a captive audience, immersing myself in each author's world until it felt familiar. And the more I read, the further I travelled, the more my eyes were opened. Eventually I came to feel that the complex world of academic non-fiction I'd explored in my youth was merely one ideological megacity on a vast planet of unthinkably diverse ideas and experiences.

That, to me, is the ultimate power of non-fiction: it allows us to look at the same world through different eyes. After reading *The Warmth of Other Suns* by Isabel Wilkerson, I have never walked through New York City in the same way.

New viewpoints can be jarring, even paralysing. It's sometimes too painful to hold everyone's perspectives in mind at once. We still have to live, after all! But this is why I continue to read non-fiction, from DuBois to Didion, from Wilfrid Hodges to Wu Ming-Yi. Each book adds a new author to the cacophonous cast of characters in my head, all incessantly arguing with each other across time and place, about the nature of reality, what is valuable, and which knowledge is worth preserving and sharing.

Erica Benner
author of *Be Like the Fox*

Reading is usually a solitary activity, but it also connects us with other people, and with the non-human world that feeds and frees us from human cages. The nature I encounter out walking looks different to me from how it did before I got reading about the compassion of trees and the biography of soil; my romantic notions of nature's majesty gave way to respect, gratitude and solidarity. But I first became a non-fiction reader because I wanted to make friends, especially with people who were unfriendly to me. Growing up a conspicuous foreigner in Japan, I wanted to understand why so many people treated me like an exotic creature, pointing and saying '*Gaijin!*' as if we belonged to different species of primate. So I scoured books from my parents' shelves. They described how American warships forced Japan into 'free trade' on their terms in the nineteenth century. To mobilize the populace against western threats, Japanese politicians cobbled together a new national identity. They dredged up an ancient, incestuous myth of Japan's origin – the sun goddess Amaterasu copulated with her brother Moon – then set up a mass education system that drummed the new ethnocentric identity into schoolchildren's heads. Reading this history didn't free me from irritation at being so rudely Othered. But it did show how walls of nationality or race aren't natural but made, and gave hope that they can be unmade.

Friend-making impulses drive most of my reading. I read to understand why people who think differently do so. The child of moderate Christians, I wasn't sure about God, and didn't think any human should be anointed one; so I delved into the anthropology of religion, and read C. S. Lewis's account of why he was Christian. As a Cold War-era teenager who distrusted all Us-vs-Them ideologies, I gave both Lenin and free-market libertarianism a fair hearing, then gave up on both and started reading philosophy.

I've always liked books that give my brain a workout, or books filled with puzzles that beg me to read again. How could Machiavelli help tyrants crush free peoples, yet praise the virtues of free-spirited republics? Why does Plato's Socrates propose the rule of philosopher kings, then say that truly wise philosophers know only one thing: that they're really no wiser than others? I can't read my favourite philosophy books without physically wrestling with them, changing them as they change me. They start off clean, black ink on white pages, and end up slathered in pink green yellow purple highlights, margins bursting with scrawl. Happy books, one of my students called them. Friends. Liberators. Deathless spirits that help us, their readers, to think about where we fit in the wider cosmos, and how to be better humans.

Ananyo Bhattacharya

author of *The Man from the Future*

My reading journey began, like most do, with listening. In Calcutta, I remember pestering any adult crossing our threshold to read the Bengali nonsense verse of Sukumar Ray, a sort of Indian Edward Lear. One of Ray's poems, for example, concerns a Rube Goldberg machine that dangles delectable morsels of food in front of the wearer's face so that they are able to run incredible distances, enticed ever-forward by the appetising aroma. After my mother moved us to England, I slowly lost my ability to read and write my native language. Poetry in translation is, like Guinness outside Dublin, just a shadow of the real thing, so I've recently once more started hounding relatives to read Ray's verses to me again.

When the symbols on the page started at last forming into words, I read for pleasure as everyone should. And later there were comics. Tintin and Asterix and superheroes gave way to Gaiman, Moore and Ennis.

By ten, I think, science fiction had entranced me – the classics of the American Golden Age and John Christopher's 'tripods' trilogy are among the works I've pressed into my children's hands. I still don't know whether I fell in love with science because of the likes of Asimov and Heinlein or whether a fascination with science drove me to read those who imagined its possibilities best. Either way, those books set me off on the meandering path between science and scribbling that I'm still on today.

A foreigner's insecurity led me to read the Western canon with the urgency of an outsider determined to understand the alien culture of their new home. The parallels between the *Iliad* and the *Mahabharata* or the *Odyssey* and the *Ramayana* might have made for a fun comparative literature thesis. Instead, I ended up shivering in a cold room trying to germinate and grow recalcitrant crystals of protein.

For around a decade, immersed in science, I would read only stories to escape the rigours of the lab – almost anything as long as it was made up. Later, after embarking on another career, this time in journalism, I returned to facts and logic, science and philosophy.

The only pattern I can find in all that ceaseless reading is that one book invariably led to another, and I felt there would never be the time to read all that I wanted and *needed* to. And perhaps *that* is why we read; because it is a habit, an addiction, a compulsion, an affliction and a necessity. Like drawing breath.

James Bridle
author of *Ways of Being*

For a few years I've kept a list of every book I've read – and not only those I've actually finished, which isn't always the important detail. It turns out I average about fifty a year. But the most striking thing that occurs to me, reviewing the list, is what's omitted. There's plenty I can't remember reading – detective novels, as much as I enjoy them, don't stay in the mind, and that's a good thing, permitting comfortable re-readings – but there's so much else I've read too, and just as voraciously: essays, magazine articles, scientific papers, exhibition texts, scraps of journals, tweets, blog posts, signs, the labels on electronic goods and the backs of toilet cleaner. A world of texts, all informative, all full of meaning, all waiting to be read.

As a teenager, I came across a quotation in Albert Hourani's *A History of the Arab Peoples* that I admired so much I wrote it out by hand and pinned it to my bedroom wall. It is an extract from a text by the twelfth century Baghdadi scholar 'Abd al-Latif, on the scholar as the ideal type of person. In part, it read: 'One should read histories, study biographies and the experiences of nations. By doing this, it will be as though, in his short life space, he lived contemporaneously with peoples of the past, was on intimate terms with them, and knew the good and the bad among them.' I've come to realize that this applies to every kind of reading: every text a telegram, a scrap of news, a missive from another life and realm of experience, however quotidian, humble, or esoteric. I want to know everything, and I want to walk alongside everyone, in the past and the present, and hear their stories. To be on intimate terms with the world.

Al-Latif also wrote: 'When you read a book, make every effort to learn it by heart and master its meaning. Imagine the book to have disappeared and that you can dispense with it, unaffected by its loss.' I confess I haven't learned much by heart, but I think the act of reading is more about navigating a territory in order to grasp it on another level: to know it like a home, rather than a map, or gaz-etteer. I don't remember every road I've ever walked down, but I am changed by the journey, and my sense of the world, and my place in it, changes too.

Clare Carlisle

author of *Philosopher of the Heart*

Most books contain years of their author's life, compressed to an inch or so between the covers. Writers of biography or history, for example, must spend hundreds of hours researching, reading, selecting and storytelling. They visit libraries and archives, chasing their subject through a labyrinth of books and articles and websites. They sit in stations and airports, on trains and planes, trying to write. They walk around thinking about their sentences; they get up in the night to rearrange their paragraphs. Some days they feel exhausted or depressed by the whole thing. For months and months they talk to friends and partners, editors and colleagues, about the book that is slowly coming into being.

Being an author who has done all these things, I feel a sort of amazement at the difference between a book that is written and a book that is read. All those hours of consciousness, all those miles travelled, are poured into something no larger than a box of fried chicken, no heavier than a teapot – a humble object that will spend just a short time in its reader's hands.

Before I became an author I worked as a waitress. Though I liked the job, I sometimes envied the customers, who could sit and enjoy the things I brought them. When I worked in a coffee shop I would wish I was free to hang out with a friend or read a magazine. When I worked in a restaurant, I would think how luxurious it would feel to be out having dinner, drinking wine, wearing a nice dress and perfume instead of my waitress clothes. That was twenty years ago, but still when I am sitting in a café I think about the fact that, in this moment, I am the lucky person who gets to enjoy my coffee, made how I like it, and a piece of cake I have chosen, while someone else is on their feet, hard at work.

To be a reader, then: how nice, how free, how fortunate! All you have to do is sit in bed with your chosen book and surf the smooth surface of those pages, which turn so easily. You can encounter in their lightest, most transparent form the ideas and people and stories that have been thoughtfully arranged there, one after the other – sentence after sentence, paragraph after paragraph, page after page – for your convenience. Without moving you can go to another city, another landscape, maybe another century. If you are reading a biography, you are meeting another human being and you will know that person, at least a little bit, for the rest of your life. And whatever kind of book you are reading, you get to rest for a while in the author's mind and share their unique way of looking at things and putting them together. In a few hours you will learn, without effort, everything this other person has laboured for years to know and understand.

Shami Chakrabarti

author of *Of Women*

Solace without sedation, education without drill and the ultimate possibility of argument without arms. We read to think, listen, understand and be entertained in an act as solitary and communal as humanity itself. We read because we are human and to be able to read is the most important life skill that connects us with the aspirations, experience and wisdom of people all over the world. This includes those no longer around and those yet to come.

Whether reading the room with empathy or reading the riot act to exert power, reading is never passive. Without active and ceaseless reading, even the best of laws will be consigned to the dead letter of a sealed book. Literacy of all kinds is key to democracy itself. That is why library closures and book burning are always synonymous with oppression.

When I was small my mother first read to me and then taught me to read before I was old enough to attend school. Now that she is gone, those moments are perhaps her greatest gift to her daughter. So many of us begin our journey with fairy tales and remain tellers and readers of stories throughout life. Still, in a dystopian, 'post-truth' era, it has become necessary to seek trusted sources and read widely and more deeply to distinguish fact from fiction. We can choose to nourish and fuel our minds or to read ourselves to sleep.

I write a few days after twenty-seven refugees drowned in the English Channel. The authorities on both sides of the water are engaged in a war of words and blame. Yet each has undermined the 1951 Refugee Convention for decades. How do I know this? Because I have read and re-read that precious document and not just the spin that successive governments have put on it in thought, word and deed. You are no less a refugee when they call you a 'migrant' or when, in desperation, you escape your war-torn homeland with forged papers and sinister smugglers to the nations that engaged in those same wars from afar.

I write as new laws herald voter suppression and threaten our rights to street protest and free speech in institutions of learning. From messages in bottles, to dissident pamphlets and whistle-blowing blogs, dreamers and agitators have always written in the hope of finding readers who will spread the word in whispers until it is safe to call openly for freedom, equality and justice.

We turn to history and philosophy in the fight against fascism and deliberate misinformation that denies real threats to human lives and even our continuing existence. We do not surrender to the purveyors of hate and unreason, and so we read.

Clare Chambers

author of *Intact*

When my children were small, we used to call non-fiction books 'fact books'. 'Do you want a story,' I'd ask, 'or a fact book?' Fact books were about dinosaurs, or space, or inventions; rulers, or pyramids, or rainforests. Fact books took us far away in time and place, up and down the food chain, in and out of rabbit warrens, railway tunnels, black holes. At the end of a fact book, returning back to our own house, our own time, we were changed. We had learned.

When I'm choosing for myself, most of what I read is non-fiction. As a philosopher, reading is part of my job as well as my leisure time. But it doesn't seem right to call these works of philosophy and politics 'fact books'. So much non-fiction does not contain facts; or not only facts. It is *opinions* about facts. It is *theories* that use, interpret and predict facts. And it is *arguments*: arguments about facts, opinions and theories.

Why do we want to read other people's arguments? It's not usually as simple as saying that we want to know what they think. *That someone else thinks something* is rarely reason enough to pay attention, at least not for several hundred pages. We need a greater incentive to let others' view of the world be ours for a while.

We might want to know what someone else thinks if they have experience that we lack. Reading the views of people whose lives are unlike ours can be like finding out about Jupiter or gypsum. This sort of reading is a way of reading facts: facts about what it's like to be someone else, to live in their world and share their thoughts.

But we also read the work of authors who differ from us not in their experiences but in their ideas. What do we do when we read someone with whom we predictably disagree? Do we read for the pleasure of being enraged? Do we read with the delicious anticipation of righteous indignation? Do we read so as to know what the enemy is thinking, to gain ammunition for our next attack? Or do we read because we want to *change our minds*?

It seems very odd to think that we might choose to read in order to change our minds. If we think our minds need changing, can't we just change them ourselves? And if our minds don't need changing, why take the risk of being persuaded into falsehood? And yet, despite this oddness, I often read to see if I need to change my mind. I read to learn new things, but also to test the things I think I already know.

Whether non-fiction changes your mind depends on where your mind was to start with, and on where you are willing to let it go. Reading helps when our minds are not yet made up. But perhaps we should read even more urgently when our minds are set.

Ha-Joon Chang

author of *Economics – A User's Guide*

Whether it is the heady magic-realist Colombia of Gabriel Garcia Marquez (my favourite writer, even if I can read him only in English), the murderous upper-class world of mid-twentieth-century Britain in which the hyper-logical but compassionate Hercule Poirot (my favourite fictional character) operates, the haunting worlds created by N. K. Jemisin, in which even the basic laws of the universe are unlike ours, or Douglas Adams's galactic world full of fantastical beings and comical satires, I love being immersed in a world that is so different from (yet in some ways similar to) the world I live in. But the different world doesn't have to be fictional. It could be the world of financial speculation, so deftly depicted by Charles Kindleberger in his *Manias, Panics, and Crashes*, the world of nationalistic political imaginations beautifully dissected by Benedict Anderson in *Imagined Communities*, or the world of food described with passion, sympathy and occasional sarcasm in the restaurant reviews of Jay Rayner. Or it could be a short newspaper or magazine article about something I don't know much about, whether it is about community solidarity in some impoverished neighbourhood of London or dialects of killer whale communities in the Northeast Pacific.

Reading about different worlds, often described from perspectives and experiences that are very different from mine, teaches me how there are things that I don't even know that I don't know. Whenever I finish reading a piece of writing – whether it is a long novel, a short newspaper article, or weighty non-fiction – it is as if I have lived another life, however briefly and partially.

Paul Collier
co-author of *Greed is Dead*

I read for thrills, and I am systematic about it.

The thrill comes when the surprise of reading about a new advance links with some quite different knowledge stored away in the recesses of the mind. That link becomes an insight: the process which all creative artists know. For me, it starts when a problem becomes intractable. From the mystery of dreaming, random links can miraculously crystalize through the steam of an early morning shower. The day is then spent in *flow* as the entire mind is absorbed in exploring it. Only wide reading can offer those encounters with the new.

My system starts with working through each week's *Times Literary Supplement*. Its editors span an astonishingly eclectic range of subject and opinion, and the reviews guide me into reading history, psychology, philosophy, science, anthropology: anything that takes me beyond the narrow confines of my own discipline. Reading turns into *flow*, and from there the craftsmanship of turning a new idea into a readable book is immeasurably helped by my editors at Penguin. Those wonderful orange spines scattered around our home are forged through people who guide an author into readability. A book that is a joy to read is seldom a joy to write. But the daily emails from readers, some challenging a passage that discomforted them, and many who feel their lives have been enriched, is an inspiration to battle on.

Paul Davies

author of *What's Eating the Universe?*

TO READ PERCHANCE TO DREAM

The origin of reading and writing is lost in the mists of time, but the use of symbols to convey words and concepts as a mode of cultural evolution dates back several thousand years. I still think it is something of a miracle that an array of simple shapes, appropriately arranged, almost instantly triggers in our minds a flow of meaning and emotion. An extraordinary cascade of neurological activity somehow transforms visual patterns into outrage, amusement, concern, knowledge. Is this phenomenon just a quirk of the human mind, or does it go hand-in-hand with intelligence? Is our ability to read *without thinking* related to other remarkable human traits, like our facility for music, or ironical humour? Would intelligent aliens also be able to read or, more to the point, *want* to read?

I want to read, but why? Often for the sheer joy of it – the tactile pleasure of handling a book, replete with the promise of rich pickings, the ability to browse without specifically engaging in a targeted search, thumbing through a text and spotting something interesting or even important that I would otherwise have overlooked. Even browsing bookshelves brings its own rewards; stumbling across an obscure book while looking for something else might reveal a whole new interest or line of enquiry.

Much of the time I read for the same reasons as everybody else – for the sheer delight of it, and for its practical use as a tool to access facts, jog memories, learn new ideas. But there is an additional dimension to my reading life that comes from a career in theoretical physics, for in this realm symbols take on a fascinating new power. I learned to read ordinary text so long ago that I have very little recollection of the original learning process, but learning new mathematics has continued all my life. I can observe the gradual transformation from my perusing meaningless juxtaposed symbols, through the first glimmer of understanding, to the full-blown 'Aha!' moment when the formulae and equations fall into place and speak to me. At that point, a new window opens up in my mind, a window into a world of patterns, structures and relationships that I previously never suspected even existed. I revel in the sublime joy of seeing a page of familiar equations and instantly feeling a hidden mathematical universe unfold before me.

I appreciate that, for the vast majority of people, being confronted with a page of mathematics, even when the equations are interspersed with explanatory sentences, is a mind-numbing experience. I can understand that. A chemist friend of mine once remarked, when I complained about his dry explanation of a sequence of reactions that featured pages of tedious chemical symbols, 'You see the notes, but I hear the music!' And indeed, musicians can look at a musical score and hear a melody in their heads. So it is with theoretical physics. The equations describing the great book of nature do not merely catalogue facts, but are in a very real sense art forms. The symbols are interwoven with subtle symmetries and beautiful abstract forms, reflecting the elegance inherent in the underlying laws of the universe. I value the books that contain these treasures, resplendent as they are with vectors and integrals and tensor indices and partial differential equations, texts that capture concepts which simply have no mode of expression in normal language.

The essayist Alistair Cooke famously remarked that he preferred radio to television because 'the pictures were better'. Cooke's captivating *Letters from America*, read in his own voice on BBC Radio, vividly conveyed life in the United States to British audiences. Reading a book of theoretical physics – even without diagrams – conforms with Cooke's sentiment. The pictures are better. No fancy computer-enhanced video can compete with reading, and re-reading, the actual text.

Imagination is the key to enjoying good literature. But it is also the key to good science. Scientific research is an activity that blends logic and rigorous reasoning with a free-flowing creativity. Many of my colleagues attribute their success to an ability to actually picture abstract mathematical structures such as warped spacetime or intrinsic spin in a sort of extended imagination space – a mental canvas beyond the realm of normal reflection. Like the dream world, there is a magical, ethereal quality to the world of mathematical physics. And reading provides the portal to the profound truths that lie therein.

Richard Dawkins
author of *The Blind Watchmaker*

THE LITERATURE OF SCIENCE

Doesn't it strike you as just a little bit odd that publishers, book-sellers, librarians and reviews editors tend to classify books into 'fiction versus non-fiction'? Why not 'cookery versus non-cookery'? 'gardening versus non-gardening'? 'Assyrian woodwind instruments versus everything else'? Fiction is stories about events that never happened to people who never lived. Non-fiction is everything else. It includes biography, autobiography and history – events that really happened to real people in real places. It includes science, which is stories about all that is or ever was or ever will be (as Carl Sagan put it), everything from quarks to galaxies, fossils to Fibonacci series, dinosaurs to bacteria, *habilis* to *sapiens*. As if that wasn't enough, non-fiction includes art, music, cathedrals, fashion photography, flower arranging and everything else. Everything – except things that never happened, which is the province of fiction.

We zoologists are familiar with unbalanced divisions of the world that nevertheless seem to work: 'humans versus animals', where humans actually are animals and constitute only one tiny twig buried somewhere in the massively branched tree of ten million species; 'vertebrates versus invertebrates', where vertebrates are only a sub-phylum within the phylum Chordata, and Chordata is only one among some thirty animal phyla. And of course it makes sense that the book-trade scales should be weighted towards books that people want to buy, titles that reward publishers. If there are books on Assyrian woodwind instruments they don't overburden our hypothetical balance – or the library shelf. So, assuming booksellers and publishers know their business, we are left with the undeniable fact that we all love fiction, and the not uninteresting question of why.

Why do we love to read about people who never lived, what they never said to each other, and things that never happened to them? That question belongs in critical territory where angels fear to tread, however tempted this fool may be. For I too adore fiction, and I often wonder why. Dodging the question, I shall turn to science books and why everyone should read them. As well as fiction.

Science is why you exist, in the only meaning of 'why' that ultimately makes sense. It's how you got here: about the very meaning of 'how'; about where 'here' is, and how it got to be the way it is. And the 'you' in my sentence means every you that has ever breathed, including Shakespeare and Schubert, the postman and the president 100 years hence, the dog next door, and an anonymous mosasaur hunting the Mediterranean. Except that the Med wasn't there in the Mesozoic. It was part of the larger Tethys Sea. The map of the world was different in those days, and that too is a fascinating story. Want to run the shifting world map 100 million years on when, sadly, there'll be nobody around to chart it? On those continents of the long hence, there'll be nobody to read a sonnet, no eye for a Rembrandt, no ear for a Paganini or a Liszt. But let us still exult in our ability to foresee their shape-shifted geography.

Reluctant to believe we'll all be gone? Sorry, but 100 million years is a powerful long time. We can't fathom geological time, accustomed as we are to the tinpot timescale of human history. As Brahms rightly said of a symphony, geological time is no joke. There'll be plenty of time to go extinct. Extinction has been the fate of the huge majority of species that have ever lived. In order for our descendants to defy not just time but geological Time, dodging the type of bullet that decked the dinosaurs, we shall need to be powerfully unique. Well, to be sure, we are blessed with some relevant uniquenesses. We are the only species with language – and how that got started is a scientific teaser in its own right. Consequently, ours is the only species whose knowledge is cumulative, building directly and even exponentially (at least where the all-important computer technology is concerned) on past generations; the only species with a technology that might equip a Noah-style minority to survive a global catastrophe of dinosaurian magnitude. Who could have foreseen a species of African apes capable of reaching escape velocity and hurtling out of Earth's gravity well? We are the only species with any hope of saving the planet from the fate of the dinosaurs – for an even larger comet or asteroid will, one terrible day, arrive. Worried about climate change? If not too late it will be science that saves us, the only thing that can.

But science is not just useful. Usefulness is just the start. Science is wonderful, uplifting, enthralling. Science books, if worthy of their matter, have the power to lift us above the mundane, to raise our imaginations to realms that in past centuries were surrendered to the poverty of religion. Science is, or should be, the inspiration for great literature, works to stand in the highest of our literary canons. Why has the Nobel Prize in Literature never been awarded for writing science?

I haven't made a detailed count, but the Nobel Prizes in literature have almost always gone to novelists or poets. A simple majority would have seemed appropriate, for novels really can illuminate what it is to be human. William Golding could have written a psycho-anthropological thesis, but it would have gathered dust under 'non-fiction' instead of flying off the fiction shelves as *Lord of the Flies*. The Nobel list includes a well-deserved sprinkling of philosophers and historians such as Bertrand Russell and Winston Churchill. But not a single one of the 118 prizes for literature has been awarded to a scientist. The only arguable exception was Henri Bergson (1859–1941), but he was a mystic and the very opposite of a scientist. Nowadays he is known mainly for an obscurantist tautology: life is driven by a mysterious *élan vital* – deliciously satirized in Julian Huxley's railway train propelled by *élan locomotif*. It is tragicomic to suggest that scientific literature has risen no higher than Bergson. Julian Huxley himself was a better candidate but he was easily outshone by, to name but a few writing in English, James Jeans, Carl Sagan, Lewis Thomas, J. B. S. Haldane, D'Arcy Thompson, Jacob Bronowski, Ernst Mayr, Loren Eiseley, Richard Feynman and Stephen Jay Gould. Peter Medawar stands out above all, but he won the prize for physiology, so literature too might have seemed over the top. But just read, say, *Pluto's Republic*, revel in his patrician mastery of cultivated, deeply literate wit, and wonder how the Nobel literature committee could have overlooked him.

Science is the poetry of reality. It provokes and simultaneously soothes our existential terror of deep time and intergalactic space, our bafflement in the face of evolved complexity – Darwinian life: perhaps above all the brain itself, the only object in the known universe capable of even trying to understand itself. Deployed by the Darwinian algorithm, the blind laws of physics coerced atoms of carbon, hydrogen, oxygen, nitrogen, phosphorus and other elements into sculpting a brain. A hundred trillion connections fire between 86 billion neurones, and the brain finds itself capable of mathematics, poetry and philosophy, finds itself numinously transported by a Beethoven quartet, by a Shakespeare sonnet, or by awed contemplation of the silent wastes between the stars.

> It is as if the Milky Way entered upon some cosmic dance. Swiftly the head mass becomes an enchanted loom where millions of flashing shuttles weave a dissolving pattern, always a meaningful pattern though never an abiding one; a shifting harmony of subpatterns.
> (*Sir Charles Sherrington, Nobel Prize for Physiology, 1932*)

Christopher de Hamel
author of *Meetings with Remarkable Manuscripts*

You don't have to read to enjoy a book. For seven or eight hundred years many bibliophiles have collected books for the delight of possession. There is a huge market for antiquarian and even modern books which are never read. The most expensive illuminated manuscripts in the world are mostly in languages and scripts which their buyers do not know and never expect to understand. There is even a flourishing Penguin Collectors Society, whose members would not possibly risk damage to their precious early editions by anything so unwise and hazardous as reading. The early nineteenth-century bibliophile Richard Heber said that no gentleman should be without three copies of a book, one for show, one for use, and one for borrowers. The copies for use will become disfigured and damaged and those lent will never be seen again, but the retained and unused copy is always the most precious. A book may be a tangible monument in the history of human achievement or literature, or have its place in the evolution of typography and book design, or it may have illustrations which are far more important than its text. Some very great books have no text at all. An antiquarian book is sometimes precious for its binding, which can be a work of art in its own right, or for a particular provenance in the possession of some notable collection or individual. Reading is not the primary reason for keeping such books safe. A responsible public curator would discourage a library user from ordering a copy of a book once owned by the poet John Donne, for example (there are many), for no other purpose except reading the text. Ask to see a Gutenberg Bible because you are interested in reading the Gospels and you will be shown the exit.

Most great artefacts of our culture are not now used for their original purpose. A major renaissance painting is usually no longer kept above a church altar to aid the spiritual focus of the Sacrament of the

Mass, or hung at home to remind its patrons of the appearance of someone they knew in life. A suit of armour is not used in battle; tableware from eighteenth-century Sèvres is seldom eaten off; a Tang horse is not expected to accompany the soul of the dead; we no longer need Stonehenge to measure the seasons. Books seem different, because they mostly end up in libraries rather than museums, but don't be fooled. Books are items which can be bought and sold and gathered together for the delight of their owners. We all know those irritating people who boast sanctimoniously, 'I am not really a collector – I buy books I want to read,' as if such limited appreciation were a virtue. Even worse are the neighbours who survey our shelves dubiously and inquire, 'Have you read all your books?' (Of course not, and I never will.) Reading is transitory; books endure. They can be held in the hand, touched, cradled, patted, examined, opened (carefully), closed (quickly), admired, shown and shared with friends; they can be identified, collated, measured, compared, inscribed, repaired, boxed, counted, shelved, endlessly arranged and rearranged, seen, dusted, exclaimed over, and smelled (an observation often made by people entering old libraries); they can be chased through auctions or run to earth in bookshops and carried home in triumph after nights of sleepless anxiety; they can be bequeathed, desired, competed for, rediscovered, exhibited and published, and they can be deeply sentimental to their owners; their presence can furnish a room, finance a pension fund, underpin the credentials of a university, and they can inspire children and writers by merely existing. Books can be used and enjoyed in a thousand wonderful ways that don't necessarily include reading. Here is the point, however. They could. Despite all the useful and important reasons for owning a book, you could, you actually could, if you really wanted to, read it as well. That is why books are so extraordinary.

Matthew Desmond
author of *Evicted*

The artist David Salle once said that at the most basic level the function of painting is to make the room look better. One moment, there is a wall with nothing on it. In the next, there is a de Kooning, which looks as if it may be creating its own energy, or a painting by Jenny Saville, overpowering you with its terrible beauty, or a cut-paper silhouette by Kara Walker, which haunts you long after you've turned away. If you resist the urge to explain, allowing yourself to stand naked and silent in front of the work, you have a chance to experience its full power, which is the power of creation. God power.

The best writing affects me in the same way.

I read to be amazed. I read to meet sentences that burrow themselves inside, becoming a part of me. Which is to say, I read for craft.

Of course I read to learn things, perhaps in a more anxious mode than most. I'm a social scientist by trade and, admittedly, at heart, which means I'm committed to the idea that before running on about the great problems of our day, I need to have a firm understanding of the facts, the kind that are quantifiable and the kind that aren't. I feel this gives me some licence to speak. It's not the only licence to be had – I admire the kind of people I grew up around, people who know what they know because they've stuck their head under the hood or walked the fence line – but it's the one I carry these days. I think it was the American sociologist Daniel Bell who once said that we are entitled to our own opinions but not our own facts. I try to limit the amount of daylight between the two. I'm not like those horses Montaigne identified with, who 'stumble more often on a smooth road'. I'm like those cats who stop in their tracks and paw at the path until they are sure the way is safe. I want empirical answers to empirical questions. I do my homework.

This can be hard going and tedious, I admit, but one wishes that at least those at the helm of American democracy would make a better show of it. Witness how many of our leaders openly flaunt their flight from philosophy and science and seriousness. 'George Washington in 1783 relaxed with Voltaire's letters and Locke's *On Human Understanding*,' wrote C. Wright Mills, another fine American sociologist. 'Eisenhower read cowboy tales and detective stories.' If only Mills had been around to see what happened here in 2016. At least Eisenhower read.

The US public, too, appears to be reading less and less. Our Bureau of Labor Statistics actually tracks this kind of thing, reporting that most American adults don't read for pleasure on any given day. Yet most of us are on a social media platform. We *are* reading – just not for pleasure and (for the most part) not stuff written by people who tend their sentences.

Last year, I gave up Twitter for Lent and never logged back on. I haven't yet been able to bring myself to keep scrolling through words dashed off unthinkingly when I haven't finished all of Tolstoy or Baldwin or Jane Addams. I understand the importance, and even the greatness, of a platform like Twitter. I just prefer the conversation at this table. Degas said that painting is easy unless you know what you're doing. Writing too.

If writing has an opposite, Tweeting sometimes might be it. I've borrowed this particular way of putting things from Rebecca Solnit, who wrote in her essay collection *Orwell's Roses* that 'if war has an opposite, gardens might sometimes be it.' She took care with this sentence, the 'if' and the 'sometimes' wrapping the profundity of the observation in a sugar coating of humility. There it is again: beauty and wisdom spun out of thin air.

Jared Diamond
author of *Upheaval*

SHAKESPEARE OR SHEEP?

Why do we read? I could answer this question by relating why I, Jared Diamond, read. I could rhapsodize about my pleasure in reading Shakespeare's *Hamlet*.

But, much more interesting and important than the question of why Jared Diamond reads is the question of why humans invented writing at all, and what the first scribes were writing and reading thousands of years ago. Some prehistoric inventions, such as stone tools and pottery, were easy enough to develop that they arose independently at many places and times over the globe. But writing was the most difficult major invention. There were only three occasions in world history when we can be confident that it arose in complete isolation: in Mesopotamia somewhat before 3000 BC, in China by 1300 BC, and in Mexico by 600 BC. (No, Egyptian hieroglyphics can't count as an independent invention. They arose so soon after Mesopotamian writing that we have to suspect that Egyptians derived the idea of writing from their Mesopotamian trade partners).

What were those first literate Mesopotamians reading? Was it the Gilgamesh epic, the Mesopotamian equivalent of *Hamlet*? Absolutely not! We can trace the origins of Mesopotamian writing confidently and in detail because their scribes wrote on clay, which became perfectly preserved in the dry Mesopotamian environment. Hence we know that the first Mesopotamian scribes were accountants who recorded numbers of sheep and barrels of grain for purposes of commerce and taxation. No Gilgamesh, no Shakespeare.

But please don't disparage counting sheep. They were more essential than Gilgamesh to those first agricultural and urban societies with emerging centralized governments. Mesopotamians had been using clay tokens of simple shapes to count sheep and grain for thousands of years, before they perfected Sumerian cuneiform, the world's oldest writing system to convey full texts of words, in the centuries before 3000 BC.

Another case where we can confidently specify what the first scribes were reading and writing was in Greece. The Linear B writing system of the centuries 1400–1200 BC wasn't an independent invention, but arose from a long chain of writing systems extending back through Crete's Linear A and Cretan hieroglyphic to Mesopotamia. The first Greeks to devise their own script (Linear B) for writing in an ancient form of the Greek language were the Myceneans of the Greek mainland, who traded with and then conquered Crete. We have lots of Linear B tablets preserved in the ruins of Mycenean palaces, so we know what those Myceneans were using Linear B to read. Were they poring over the great Mycenean epics, Homer's *Iliad* and *Odyssey*? Or over precursors of Plato's dialogues, Aeschylus's dramas, Sappho's poetry, and Euclid's mathematics? No way! Instead, every known Linear B tablet is an accountant's record. Rather than singing of the wrath of Achilles, those Mycenean scribes were once again counting sheep – plus wool, flax and pots. Once again, commerce and taxes came before poetry.

What about the purpose of the first writing in its two other homelands of independent origins, China and Mexico? Quick answer: we don't know, because early Chinese and Mexican cities weren't located in desert climates with good preservation of materials. As a result, the oldest preserved Chinese and Mexican texts represent obvious late stages of perfected writing systems. Our oldest preserved Chinese texts date only from around 1300 BC, more than a thousand years after the founding of Chinese cities and kingdoms that probably had writing. Those preserved texts of 1300 BC consist of religious prophecies, such as: 'If the child is born on a kang day, it will be extremely auspicious.' Surely, the first Chinese scribes had more practical messages to convey (like counting pigs and rice). Similarly, the earliest preserved Mexican writing of around

600 BC is a long complicated text carved on stone, with no mention of turkeys or corn.

In short, the oldest writing of whose purpose we can be certain – Sumerian cuneiform – was utilitarian. But, among all the respects in which we humans differ from other animal species, one is our fantastic elaboration of initially utilitarian animal productions for non-utilitarian purposes. The colour-decorated bowers by which male bowerbirds attract females, and the mounds that termites build for protection, and the songs that nightingales and whales use for communication, were respectively the precursors of the *Mona Lisa*, the Parthenon and the 'Eroica' symphony. Those human productions have evolved far beyond the original utilitarian purposes of animal art, architecture, and music. That's the broad context in which markers to count sheep evolved into the printed text of *Hamlet*.

Dennis Duncan

author of *Index, A History of the*

As far as predicting the future goes, *Johnny Mnemonic* gets a lot right. The sci-fi thriller, released in 1995 with a pre-*Matrix* Keanu Reeves in the title role, begins *Star Wars*-style, with its backstory scrolling slowly up the centre of the screen: this is the early twenty-first century; the world is dominated by corporations; and a new, fatal pandemic, its cause and cure unknown, is raging all over the world. When we meet our hero, it is early 2021. As he strides through Beijing, facemasked crowds demonstrate around him at the failure of the global leadership to combat the virus. So far, so uncanny. But not everything in the cyberpunk twenty-first century feels as prescient. It is fun to see which aspects of the film's futurology have fallen wide of the mark. Some of the absences are quaint: no one uses mobile phones; people are still sending images by fax. Some of its cool tech – like the laser whip wielded by the future-Yakuza – has yet to emerge in real life. But for me, *Johnny Mnemonic*'s most interesting prediction is the one it makes about how we will be reading in the 2020s. Johnny is a 'mnemonic agent': a data smuggler. Part of his brain (160 Gb to be precise) has been reconditioned for instant file transfer. He simply inserts a jack into a socket behind his ear and imports the data. From minidisc.

Here, then, is a thought experiment: if our own world were like Johnny's, if books were, as the film puts it, 'wet-wired brain implants', and consuming them only a matter of a few seconds' upload, would we still bother to *read* in the ordinary sense? Or, to be more precise, *which books* would we still read? Some are obvious. Where is the joy in a P. G. Wodehouse if we do not laugh – in real time – at the crystalline silliness of the sentences, or feel the giddiness as the plotting approaches its baroque peak? What is the point of a P. D. James if we do not experience its layers of clues and misdirection sequentially? In poor old Keanu's world, every who-dunnit is only spoiler.

And yet, wouldn't it be handy for other works? To have the *Chicago Manual of Style* wired into one's synapses and never split an infinitive again; to have all of Wisden pre-loaded in the memory and sweeten every conversation with a light dusting of cricket stats . . . It looks as though a simple line might be drawn: with fiction, the reading itself is an inalienable part of the pleasure. Non-fiction? Pass the minidisc.

We *use* the different types of books differently. Non-fiction *looks* different from fiction. For one thing, it has (or should have) an index – a tool which implies that the text it serves can be morselized, broken down into discrete nuggets, moments, factoids; that if you don't want to immerse yourself, to read the text in a linear way from start to finish, you can simply dip, raiding it for the information you need. So there you have it: we read non-fiction to find things out. Simple.

And yet . . . Reading is the most mercurial of verbs. We read novels and newspapers, poems and emails, tweets and roadsigns, manuals, menus and maps, and each activity has its own distinct history; each involves a different economy of attention. Each offers up a different answer to the question, 'Why do we read?' The closer we look at the idea of reading, the more the categories multiply. What, exactly, do we mean by *non-fiction*? Perhaps it was glib just then – a misdirection – to speak of style guides or sports almanacs. How about a biography, or a book of philosophy: would you take the data-transfer option, or would you prefer to read it the old-fashioned way? How about a writer's diaries – Woolf, Kafka, Anaïs Nin – or the book you're holding in your hand now? At some point, the idea of uploading begins to seem as self-defeating as mainlining poetry.

Each year I do an exercise with my students where we look at the brief opening chapter of Dickens's *Hard Times*. 'Now, what I want is, Facts. Teach these boys and girls nothing but Facts. Facts alone are wanted in life.' How can we tell, I ask, that this model of education is being sent up? What are the cues – the little winks between Dickens and us – that let us know that the unnamed speaker is a monster or a buffoon, that facts most certainly are *not* the sole basis of a sound education, that the scene is being set for a hard lesson in the richness of real life? Repetition, exaggeration, irony, caricature: the sense of ridicule in these four short paragraphs bursts from every phrase. The person expressing these views, in his 'inflexible, dry, and dictatorial' voice, is made to seem contemptible. Dickens knows – and he knows that we know – that there is more to learning than facts.

Think about a popular history book, a memoir, a piece of long-form journalism. How much of it could truly be described as *information*? Just because it's non-fiction doesn't mean it's all fact. There is a nice quip, usually attributed to John Updike, that runs: 'Most biographies are just novels with indexes.' He means, of course, that biography as a genre can't be trusted. It looks like fact – it has indexes! – but really, says Updike, it is, more often than not, partial, unreliable, made up. Besides, in non-fiction there is argument, demonstration, opinion, sometimes even style. You may be reading this now and violently shaking your head, cursing me under your breath. That's OK. Really. Reading, even (perhaps *especially*) reading non-fiction, is a conversation. It is time spent in dialogue with the author, agreeing or disagreeing, marking the cumulative stations of the argument, parsing its ideas, integrating them with one's own knowledge, one's own perceptions and experiences. 'Read, mark, learn, and inwardly digest,' counselled Thomas Cranmer. The learning cannot happen without the digestion.

When we read to find things out, then, we also do so for the same reasons that we read novels: for pleasure, for leisure, to pass the time, because we enjoy the company of the person we meet on the page. And not only that, but these motives are indivisible: we find things out *because* of the experience of the act of reading. Non-fiction readers are not little vessels, like the pupils in Gradgrind's classroom, waiting passively to have 'imperial gallons of facts poured into them until they are full to the brim'. Nor could they ever be Johnny Mnemonics, uploading wisdom till they reach capacity. The future of reading looks safe for the time being.

George Dyson
author of *Analogia*

THE TALE OF PETER RABBIT

In the library of living things, books are written in a four-letter alphabet and limited to a vocabulary of twenty words. The authors convey their multi-dimensional experience by mapping it to one-dimensional strings. The library is unbounded, with new volumes added for the next generation of creatures to read.

The Just-So Story, told by evolutionary biologists, is that the rabbits – or primates sitting around the campfire – who listen to the tale of Peter Rabbit and his adventures in Mr McGregor's garden out-survive the rabbits who don't. 'Your father had an accident there; he was put in a pie by Mrs McGregor,' Peter's mother warns. We read as if our lives depend upon it, because they do.

David Edgerton
author of *The Rise and Fall of the British Nation*

The writer George Orwell once estimated that even he spent less money on books than on tobacco. Today, most writers probably spend more time on the addictive written social media than on books. They sustain themselves not with drags from a Marlboro or a Gauloise, but with word shots from Twitter.

We can barely operate without written words: street signs, indicator boards, or texts and emails telling us what to do. Our telephones have been turned into personal telegraphs pumping out reconstituted pixelated words. TV channels subtitle in their own language. The written word, once sacred, is the banal alpha and omega of our world. So ubiquitous are words that they are no more noticeable than the air we breathe, only apparent when some words usually spoken only in privacy appear, like a gust of cold wind or a wall of tropical air.

Why are written words so powerful? It is because words once written can be consumed again and again, without interfering with other words. Imagine a railway station in which all the necessary information had to be given orally. 'This is platform one' would have to be repeated again and again and would be inaudible because of another voice intoning 'This is platform two'. Aurally controlled stations would descend into a cacophony of white noise. By contrast, written information can be put up just once and be lucid to all and sundry.

More than that, permanent written words can be easily copied, whether by hand or machine. Even today, the relative cheapness of copying words matters – hence the rise of the text message, and Twitter, and Facebook and all the rest of the new text of our newly logocentric world.

But it is not just the cheapness of the reproduced word that matters, but the speed at which we process it. We read faster than we speak, or can listen, perhaps twice as fast. A fifty-minute TV documentary has perhaps 2,000 words in it, many repeated. A radio documentary of the same length might have 5,000. But an average person can read 10,000 words in the same time. Of course, sound and images add to the word content, but how much exactly? Few pictures, even moving ones, are worth the clichéd thousand words. Indeed, there are too many documentaries, talks and even seminars we could substitute by looking up an entry or two in Wikipedia.

In the old days, broadcasters, and newspapers, could lavish money on their words, but today the price per word a freelance journalist might get is much lower than forty years ago; budgets for documentaries are very much lower too. Because book writing is inherently more economical than making a TV programme, as costs are squeezed, we would expect the quality gap between the book and the broadcast to increase. And indeed, it is now very wide.

The book, and the few magazines and newspapers which sustain large paying readerships, and a few specialized and committed journals, are now producing work of radically different quality from the mass of the written word, and the broadcast word.

That is why, in a world where stored image and sound is so available, the book still rules. It is not a matter of cultural inertia, of the power of a literary elite, but of the economics of quality information. Reading is not only a faster way of acquiring information – it provides better quality, and indeed a very much richer range of opinion, too. Recorded lectures, films, online courses of all sorts remain inadequate compared to the book. Furthermore, without the world of reading underpinning them, the lectures and films would not be what they are. The producers and directors of films and TV do not learn from other films or TV programmes, they learn from books. They write books, too.

Yet the written word can be tiresome. What a blessed relief to hear a poem spoken, a play performed, a story told, or even to find a restaurant where the bill of fare is conveyed in conversation. We want to learn not from manuals or videos but by observing and listening. Students have never just read for a degree, they need in-real-life lecturers to interact with, even if, as their title suggests, they too get their knowledge from reading.

There is, however, no escape. In this new world we read because we must. And, to understand this and much more about it, we must still read books.

Jordan Ellenberg
author of *Shape*

Sometimes, for a change of scene, I'll set up shop in one of the small, wire-framed cubicles in the college library and work on mathematics there. My practice, when I do this, is to take a break from time to time and pick out a book from the nearby shelves to look at. I bring the book back to my cubicle and give it at least half an hour of my time.

What the book is about depends on the section of the library I've chosen to sit in. Once it was a bound volume of graphic propaganda posters dropped by Nazi planes on advancing US troops. Once it was a lexicon of the Ho-Chunk language. Once it was a book from 1936 about the perilous state of American mental health, called *Why Men Fail*.

I once asked a librarian how many of the books in our library would never be checked out again. She said it was hard to even estimate, but she was sure it was at least half. You can guess, wandering the shelves, which ones seem in danger of being shelved for ever. That's how I pick out which books to look at. I've trained myself to let the books that don't catch the eye catch my eye. I pick the ones that look lonely.

When asked, 'Why do we read?' there's a custom of taking the question to be, 'What's in it for us?' I am more interested in what's in it for the book. A book needs us more than we need it. Without us, it doesn't exist. More precisely, it exists only as an inert lump of organic matter, a state of being we describe as 'no longer with us' when we or our friends finally attain it.

This way of looking at things has helped keep me from hoarding. If the book is there to do something for me, I feel compelled to keep it around – I might *need* that favour. But if we are here to serve the book, then we're punishing the book by keeping it stuck unread on our shelves. Give it away, set it free, let it find someone who treats it right.

Don't read a book because everybody else is reading it. That book doesn't need you. Don't read for self-improvement. You are fine as you are. Read for the sake of the lonely book, which can still be with us a little longer, if we are willing to be with it.

Richard J. Evans
author of *The Hitler Conspiracies*

In Bernhard Schlink's prizewinning novel *The Reader*, set in the late 1950s and 1960s, Hanna Schmitz, a German tram-conductor in her thirties, begins an affair with Michael Berg, a teenager, in which she gets him to read to her from the classics before they have sex. Some years later, he learns that she was a guard at Auschwitz who was a party to horrific crimes. During her trial, it emerges that she is illiterate; she wanted him to read out loud to her because she could not read herself. Sent to prison as a war criminal, she fills her time by learning to read, eventually discovering the full details of the Holocaust from books by survivors like Primo Levi and Elie Wiesel. On the day of her release from imprisonment in 1983, she kills herself in remorse at her crimes.

The Reader was a best-seller in Germany following its publication in 1995. It was translated into forty-five languages and has been widely used in teaching the Holocaust. In 2008 it was turned into a film starring Kate Winslet, who won an Oscar for her performance. And yet, for all its subtlety, it rests on a fundamental premise that is as dubious as it is disturbing. For one thing, illiteracy was almost unknown in Germany in the 1930s and 1940s, and just as unlikely in the German-speaking community in Romania, where the novel actually places Hanna's childhood. Far more importantly, however, it implies that it was her inability to read that enabled her to become a Holocaust perpetrator. As soon as she finally does learn to read, she realizes for the first time the enormity of what she has done, and is unable to live with it.

Ordinary Germans in the 1930s and 1940s were not ignorant of the regime's visceral and murderous antisemitism, which was broadcast to them by every means of propaganda and indoctrination available to it, from the education system to the Hitler Youth, from radio and cinema to speeches and films. You did not have to be able to read to know about it. More than that, the perpetrators of the mass murder of Europe's Jews were in many cases highly educated. Indeed, the higher up you go in the hierarchy of the SS, the organization that carried out the Holocaust, the more likely you are to find men with advanced educational qualifications. Possession of a doctorate did not stop Josef Mengele from 'selecting' Jewish victims for gassing at Auschwitz or carrying out terrible medical experiments on some of them in the name of science. Ultimately, the implicit claim that ignorance and lack of education are what allowed people to commit war crimes and atrocities is a kind of exculpation. The ability to read in itself does not make you morally upright or responsible.

Some people read in order to confirm or deepen their prejudices, like most readers in Nazi Germany of Hitler's *Mein Kampf* or the infamous antisemitic forgery *The Protocols of the Elders of Zion*; some read so that they can assimilate the ideology of a dictatorial state, like the readers in Stalin's Soviet Union of the *Short-Course History of the Communist Party of the Soviet Union (Bolsheviks)*, and keep themselves from being accused of 'deviationism'. Some read simply to gain information, a purpose that encompasses an almost infinite variety of motives; some read in order to transport themselves in the imagination to another world, whether factual or fictional, where they can escape from the present day. We might read books or essays or articles or blogs or social media posts in order to make us think, to challenge our assumptions about the world, about life, its nature and its possible purposes. We read notices, signs and other brief communications to negotiate the challenges and vagaries of our daily existence. But just as important as why we read is how we read.

Reading is not just a passive assimilation of the words on the printed page, or, at least, it shouldn't be. Of course, there are many people who think it is. When governments come to consider setting books for school students to read, for example, they seem to think that the students are empty vessels into which the books' words will simply be poured. The British Prime Minister David Cameron recommended Henrietta Marshall's 1905 history book *Our Island Story* because he seems to have regarded it as an engaging narrative of British or, rather, English history that would fill school pupils with patriotic enthusiasm. If you read it critically, however, you will quickly realize it's a compendium of myths and moral judgements that doesn't explain much about the past. Written at the height of Edwardian imperialism, it purveys attitudes and assessments that would in no way be generally acceptable today. As the historian Amanda Vickery has remarked, 'To recommend *Our Island Story* as a textbook for 9- to 12-year-olds is like relying on Mel Gibson for the history of Scotland.' Mel Gibson's portrayal of the Scottish Middle Ages in the movie *Braveheart* may be fun to watch, but accurate it most certainly is not.

Reading with the intention of interrogating the text and critically assessing what it purveys has become more urgent than ever in the age of the internet. We now live in a world of communication that's awash with conspiracy theories and fake news, and, if we're not to be swept away by all of it, we need to approach the written text, whether it's on Twitter or Facebook or on a website or in a blog, with our critical faculties working at full stretch. Lies and falsehoods are routinely disseminated across the media and the internet, often in short fake news reports or social media posts, and so widely believed that it seems impossible to dislodge them from the minds of those who have assimilated them. The written word remains the most powerful tool for countering them, for presenting the evidence, and for debunking false claims and 'alternative facts'.

Seb Falk
author of *The Light Ages*

As Dan Brown's multimillion-selling thriller *The Da Vinci Code* comes towards its white-knuckle climax, the hero, legendary symbologist Robert Langdon, has to solve a tricky riddle to open the mysterious cryptex. The first line, he soon realizes, refers to Sir Isaac Newton; but the rest is harder. The riddle challenges him to identify 'the orb that ought be on his tomb'. At first Langdon is clueless: among the many planets and constellations dotted above the black marble sarcophagus, what could possibly be missing? Fortunately, Brown does not keep us in suspense for long. 'The orb that ought be on Newton's tomb could be none other than the Rosy apple that fell from heaven, struck Newton on the head, and inspired his life's work.' Work which, Brown is keen to emphasize, 'incurred the wrath' of a malevolent Catholic Church.

History of science is more popular than ever. The tale of humanity's greatest achievements, of astounding progress occasionally tempered by extraordinary errors: its attraction is obvious. A catalogue of complex theories could be dry, but like all history it has biography at its heart. Not only are we travelling into the past, we're peering into the lives of some of the most interesting and creative people who ever lived. Who wouldn't want to read about that?

A problem arises, however, when biography slips into hagiography. The story of Newton's apple turns out to be legend, a small seed of truth buried in juicy embellishment. Newton himself told the story later in life. 'The notion of gravitation,' his friend and biographer William Stukeley wrote, 'was occasion'd by the fall of an apple, as he sat in a contemplative mood.' This apparently took place in 1665, when the twenty-two-year-old Newton was in his Lincolnshire garden, a refugee from plague-ravaged Cambridge. During two years of lockdown, Newton himself later asserted, he found the answers to a multitude of questions in maths and physics. 'For in those days,' he mused half a century later, 'I was in the prime of my age for invention & minded Mathematicks & Philosophy more than at any time since.'

The tale of what has become known as Newton's *annus mirabilis* fits perfectly with how we might imagine scientific discovery: a blinding flash of inspiration for a lone genius, as Nature herself knocks him on the head and all the pieces of the puzzle fall into place. (Never mind that the knocking on the head part was a nineteenth-century addition to the tale.) The story hides Newton's dependence on other thinkers, such as Descartes, Kepler and Hooke. Newton was reluctant to acknowledge them, but even he admitted, with a turn of phrase popular from the Middle Ages, that he was 'standing on the shoulders of giants'. The story also obscures the painstaking processes of development: Newton's *Principia*, in which, as he proudly declared, 'I demonstrate the frame of the System of the World', was not published for more than twenty years after his retreat to Lincolnshire.

Reading the history of science, we can go beyond simply critiquing myths such as these: we can ask ourselves what these myths might mean, or what they were intended to mean. What did Newton wish to suggest by telling his story of the apple? It had a religious connotation – Dan Brown was right about that much. But it does not signify the banishment of faith from science – far from it. Newton himself wrote that it was the business of natural philosophy to 'discourse of God'. God was explicitly present in Isaac's universe: his faith led him to attempt to reconstruct the designs of Solomon's temple, and to ascribe seven colours to the rainbow in his search for divine harmony. For him, then, the apple was a return to the Garden of Eden, to the Tree of Knowledge. For his followers, Newton was a new Adam, revealing the laws of Nature lost at the Fall.

We need such close readings to puncture the easy myths. The pastoral image of an English gentleman scholar in his orchard might be reassuring, when science so often conjures images of genetically modified crops or test-tube viruses; but it is, at best, misleading. To update it, historians learn how to read varied sources of information – not just stories but theories, not just texts but tables, diagrams and instruments: the prism Newton purchased at the fair just outside Cambridge, or the pioneering reflecting telescope he made. His story now turns out to extend far beyond Lincolnshire: the philosopher who never left England depended for his discoveries on global networks of scientific communication, bringing him data on tidal flows in the Pacific or reports of comets over Brazil. The historian's craft is to read these raw materials, and shape them into an account just as appealing as the familiar fairy tales.

Yet those old tales remain irresistible. Even people unaware of Newton's staggering contributions in optics, calculus or celestial dynamics (not to mention his passion for alchemy or ancient history) know the story of the falling apple. Publicized in Romantic histories from the nineteenth century, it has remained popular ever since. It seemingly speaks to our deepest sense of wonder at what the human mind can accomplish.

The tourists who flock to Trinity College, Cambridge, may be disappointed to discover that the apple tree outside the main gate is not the one Newton sat beneath. But just inside the college they will find Newton himself: this devout (if unorthodox) Christian is memorialized in marble in the college chapel. William Wordsworth perfectly encapsulated his contemplative expression – as well as that Romantic sense of Newton's genius – when he described

> The antechapel where the statue stood
> Of Newton with his prism and silent face,
> The marble index of a mind for ever
> Voyaging through strange seas of Thought, alone.

While historians might bemoan Wordsworth's distorted image of a solo journey of scientific discovery, we can only admire his poetic vision. The challenge is to make some of the most complex ideas ever conceived just as alive as the people who thought them. If we solve that riddle, we can come closer to an account, both truthful and compelling, of humanity's collective quest to unlock the endless secrets of the cosmos.

Niall Ferguson
author of *Doom*

In an article published in the *Philosophical Quarterly* in 2003, the Oxford philosopher Nick Bostrom proposed that 'we are almost certainly living in a computer simulation'. A good example of Richard Dawkins's concept of the 'meme' or 'mind virus', this idea proved highly contagious, with Elon Musk, the founder of Tesla and SpaceX, and Neil deGrasse Tyson, the director of Hayden Planetarium, among the super-spreaders. Of course, Bostrom was merely expressing in academic language what the movie *The Matrix* had depicted cinematically four years before.

I take a different view. My view is that life is most probably the random result of chemical and evolutionary processes, because it is mostly far too boring to have been invented by the kind of intelligence that would be capable of devising such a large-scale and complex simulation. Rather, it is literature that is the simulation. We read both fiction and non-fiction to experience imaginatively lives other than our own. This inner experience – our participation in the simulation – then enhances our own otherwise dull and repetitive lives.

Although there are forms of entertainment that require less imaginative effort – cinema, television, computer games, and now the promised 'metaverse' of virtual and augmented reality – in practice all of these are inferior to reading. The reason is that the various 'information technologies' invented in the past century leave altogether too little to the imagination, whereas literature demands that you infer entire worlds from black symbols on a white page. While many people lazily prefer movies and games to books, they unwittingly stultify themselves by giving their brains too little work to do. Of course, one expends less energy being carried in a litter than in walking or running, but there is a reason – aside from their increasing weight – why we encourage our children to use their own legs.

As a boy, I read as much as I could. I would borrow the maximum number of books from the Carnegie Public Library in Ayr – five, as I recall – and devour them one by one. Fiction was my first love, but as a teenager I came also to appreciate the historians who were capable of resurrecting the events and experiences of the past. I vividly remember my first encounter with A. J. P. Taylor, whose illustrated history of the First World War my parents owned. That was the beginning of many years of deeply satisfying reading, as Taylor was a master of English prose on a par with George Orwell. His *Struggle for Mastery in Europe* remains a masterpiece of historical writing, now almost entirely neglected. His reviews and essays put today's *epigoni* to shame.

I still read this way. Over the past two years, I have leafed my way gleefully through the novels of Walter Scott, which have given me such intense yet prolonged pleasure that I dread getting to the end of them, even more than I dreaded the last pages of Dickens's incomplete *Mystery of Edwin Drood*. What is it that makes Waverley such a work of genius? I think it is the way the reader, like the youthful protagonist whose surname furnishes the series title, is abruptly catapulted from sleepy, bucolic England into the turmoil of Scotland on the eve of the 1745 Jacobite Rebellion, and then introduced to a cast of characters so vivacious that they seem to dance off the page. Like Dickens, whom the English find easier, Scott never lost his touch. I have only just finished *Redgauntlet*, and I find myself almost in mourning for the impetuous Darsie Latimer and the alluring lady of the Green Mantle. It staggers me to think that I was warned off Scott as a boy. The man who invented the historical novel and inspired all the great continental authors in that genre – including Tolstoy – should be required reading in every school in Scotland.

Thanks to Scott, I now have the beginnings of an answer to one of the great historical puzzles. How did Scotland go, in just sixty years, from being Afghanistan in the early eighteenth century – complete with warring mountain tribes and blinkered lowland theocrats – to being the cradle of the Enlightenment, the most dynamic economy in the world, and the coal-burning, steam-driven powerhouse of the

British Empire? Thanks to Scott, more importantly, I have also made the acquaintance of Cosmo Comyne Bradwardine, Baron of Tully-Veolan, one of the most irresistible characters in all of fiction.

Literature is the simulation, then: the true and unsurpassable 'immersive experience'. Yet there is a further reason to read, and that is the way the simulation lives on in the memory, shaping and enriching all our subsequent encounters with reality. After he retired, my father devoted much time to following in the footsteps of his beloved Robert Louis Stevenson, an enthusiasm that took him as far as the South Sea islands. In the nine months between my leaving the Glasgow Academy and matriculating at Oxford, I did something similar. First, I retraced the Spanish steps of Laurie Lee in *As I Walked Out One Midsummer Morning*. Then I reenacted Jack Kerouac's *On the Road* with my Canadian cousin Colin, a journey that culminated, hazily, in the Floating Gardens of Xochimilco.

Literature not only furnishes the augmentation of reality, ensuring that no outburst of snobbery or of jealousy is without its Proustian resonance. By furnishing a kind of map and directions, it also permits the reader to relive the simulation himself.

In short, we are almost certainly not living in a computer simulation. But we can, if we choose, live in a literary simulation. I chose to do so long ago. And I shall, I trust, die reading.

Nicci Gerrard

author of *What Dementia Teaches Us about Love*

Lining the stairwell of my house are dozens of framed pictures that I've collected over the years of women reading: women from long ago and now, in gowns, in jeans, naked, on sofas, in bed, in boats, by water, lying in a bath, sitting under a tree, an umbrella, a lamp and darkness all round, sitting at a window, standing arrested with one hand on the back of a chair and the other holding a book. Women looking away from the painter at the words they are reading. In some of the pictures, they look dreamy and lost in the world of the book; in others there is an expression of fierce concentration on their faces. These ones remind me of the photograph I have in my study of one of my daughters, who struggled to read because of her dyslexia, hunched over a book, purposeful and intensely focused.

Because, while reading can mean imaginative escape and self-loss, it can also mean endeavour and a kind of hard labour of the mind. Sometimes when I read, I can almost feel my ageing, forgetting brain fizz and hiss. Cracks of light, new ways of thinking about old ideas, a sense of an order being brought to things that had seemed messy. There are some books I've read (recent examples include Svetlana Alexievich's flaying account of Russian women in the Second World War, *The Unwomanly Face of War*, Andrew Solomon's magnificent and humane exploration of depression, *The Noonday Demon*, and his *Far from the Tree*, Marion Coutt's stunning memoir of the time between her husband's diagnosis of a brain tumour and his death, *The Iceberg*) that are nerve-tingling reminders of the power of words to expand thoughts and feelings. The experience is electrifying, exhilarating and almost hurtful: the doors of the mind heave open.

I visited a friend in hospital when he was hours away from death, and I read to him. It felt like a solace (to him I hope, certainly to me), but also perhaps a way of maintaining his connection to the world right until he crossed the threshold. He was a writer, a lifelong and ardent reader; words were what he lived by and for, and how he gave shape to his world.

I read to my blind mother nowadays, just as decades ago she used to read to me. I read to my father during his months of slow-motion dying of dementia. I don't know how much he heard or understood, but sometimes this old man, who seemed to have lost everything, all words and all understanding, lifted his head and joined in with the poems he used to know. It was like a thread leading him out of the ruined labyrinth of the self, briefly back into the world.

A friend of mind with advancing dementia puts texts on the wall to read from: she walks up and down her room while reciting the words she's chosen: hanging on to her receding self, refusing to let go.

Like the women on my wall, I read wherever I find myself. I read for pleasure, for adventure, for knowledge, for stories, for company, for reassurance, for challenge, for meaning, for glimpses into other imaginations, for the boundaries of the self to dissolve. And sometimes I read as a way of keeping a grip on the world, a grip on myself in the world, a tiny speck in the rushing darkness that I am. Hold fast. Reading for my life, I guess.

Gerd Gigerenzer

author of *How to Stay Smart in a Smart World*

If you ask friends why they read, they might say, 'It's a nice way to relax', 'to escape from being bombarded by advertisements and television', or 'as a teacher, I read to save my sanity after grading essays.' We take pleasure in reading by creating an enclosed space and having a quiet time alone: me and my book. Yet that solitude was not always the idea behind reading.

For millennia, people have been reading. The Ancient Greeks read, and so did the monks in the Middle Ages and the educated aristocracy. Yet they did not read silently, as we do today. Reading meant reading aloud to someone else. Thus, reading at that time resembled audio books, although not quite. Unlike audio books, reading aloud creates or strengthens a social bond between the person who reads and the one who listens. It also offers people a respite from pain and suffering, such as when reading to those who are sick or dying.

Building social ties is the great benefit of reading aloud, but not the only one. A number of experiments have shown that reading aloud improves recall of the content compared with silent reading. Even silently mouthing the words makes these stick better in the mind, although not to the same degree. People seem to be intuitively aware of this positive effect. For instance, when it is hard to understand a recipe or an instruction, many spontaneously begin to read it aloud to facilitate comprehension.

Why then did reading become a silent, solo activity? According to Paul Saenger, a curator of rare books at the Newberry Library, Chicago, a change in writing, namely the introduction of empty spaces between words, led to the development of silent reading. Back in the days of Ancient Greece and Rome, sentences were written with one word attached to the next one. The task of the person reading aloud was to separate the words first in their minds, then with their voice. Once words became separated in Europe in the seventh and eighth centuries by Irish scribes when they copied manuscripts, silent reading was facilitated. Modern readers might ask why it took so long for this change that made reading easier for everyone. But the idea that everyone should be able to read was foreign to a world in which an elite was used to dictating what the rest should know and believe. Reading meant access to knowledge, and literacy of the hoi polloi a danger to the rule of authority.

Although we think today of reading as a silent, private activity, reading aloud never really stopped. Parents read bedtime stories to their children, lovers read to each other, religious leaders read from sacred books to their community, and pilots read aloud the items in their checklists before taking off. Reading to children fosters language learning better than showing them commercial videos such as 'Baby Einstein' and 'Brainy Baby', and having items on a checklist read aloud is essential for the safety of passengers in a plane or patients on the operating table. But reading silently has a crucial advantage: speed. We can read a text much more quickly, or even gloss over it, if we do not have to articulate the individual words. The techniques of speed-reading embody the value of 'the faster the better', which is alien to reading aloud, yet rushing through twenty to thirty words per second does not really allow for similar comprehension as when reading at a normal pace.

Finally, consider a peculiar phenomenon. People talk about books they have not read. That would have been quite natural in the age of reading aloud, where the listener could trust that the reader had not distorted the text. Yet the same tendency to trust occurs when we hear someone talking about the content of a book, without reading aloud the actual text. Even in the sciences, quite a few authors do not read the books or articles they write about. Two electrical engineers from UCLA, M. V. Simkin and V. P. Roychowdhury, studied how often errors in citation lists are passed on from paper to paper, indicating that the authors have not read what they cite, and concluded that four out of five authors do not do their homework. The general problem is that authors rely on hearsay or on what others have written, and do not make the effort to read the original sources. Some of the best-known but false stories in the social sciences resulted from this reluctance to read. For instance, in *An Odd Kind of Fame*, Malcom Macmillan looks at the famous case of Phineas Gage, the railway worker who in 1848 survived a severe accident when a tempering iron went through his skull. Macmillan shows how the few contemporary documents about Gage have been twisted into claims to support a large range of views, from phrenology to Damasio's 'somatic marker' hypothesis. Rarely, he concludes, did anyone take the effort to read the few, easily accessible original documents. These authors are not the only ones who buy into what others say instead of reading the sources. Word-of-mouth is not the same as reading aloud, but it seems to elicit similar levels of trust in the source.

Trust is an essential component of reading. When being read to aloud, the listener has to trust the speaker; when reading silently, the reader has to trust the author. The reader's trust relates to competence – whether the author understands the topic they are writing about – but also to motivation, that is, the author's intention behind the text. Determining whether one can trust an author requires certain skills, particularly in the age of online reading and fake news. These skills, however, are rarely taught. As studies have documented, the great majority of digital natives do not know how to check the trustworthiness of websites and posts, cannot tell hidden ads from real news online, and are taken in by the design of a website. Reading broadly and continually is a good antidote to being led astray by a single wrong source and is the *sine qua non* for a functioning democracy. It cultivates citizens with a critical mind who can argue with and stand up to authorities. In this sense, extensive reading is an obligation, even a moral duty.

Malcolm Gladwell
author of *The Bomber Mafia*

People often talk of reading fiction as a pathway to empathy: that the process of being immersed in the thoughts and feelings and motivations of characters in a story serves as a kind of rehearsal for understanding the inner lives of people in the real world. I've always thought something similar happens when one reads a work of non-fiction: that being immersed in a history book or a good argument of one sort or another gives you a fascinating window into how the writer thinks.

Recently I began reading Stephen Talty's *The Good Assassin*, about the hunt for the Nazi war criminal called the Butcher of Latvia. Two chapters in, I already had a score of questions in my mind for Talty. We meet, in the opening pages, the person I assume will be the hero: a Mossad agent named Mio. Did Talty meet Mio? It doesn't sound like he did. But the way he brings Mio to life in a few short paragraphs is nothing short of magical. Those few sentences made me want to meet Talty, to figure how where his gifts for re-creation come from. Then we meet the villain: Herbert Cukurs. My instinct would have been to start with the villain and then introduce the hero. Talty did the opposite: it made me wonder. Why? Is that better? What is different about Talty that makes him think that hero to villain is more compelling than villain to hero? Should I try that next time? These sound like questions about the craft of writing. But they are more than that. They are the writer's philosophy and intentions.

Ever since I was a child, I've thought that the way someone told a story *said* something about them. My father began stories at a random point, forgot key details, hemmed and hawed through the critical middle bits, then charmed his way out of trouble with a lot of artful self-deprecation. That, I understood right from the beginning, was the essence of my father. He was a mathematician. His governing assumption was that it really didn't matter how you reached the conclusion; what mattered was that you got there, in the end, one way or the other. Mind you, I didn't think that his was an example that I wanted to follow. My mother and I used to sit and silently squirm in embarrassment when my father backed himself into some narrative cul de sac. We – my mother and I – are convinced that it really does matter how you get there. We make lists and plans and follow them dutifully, and study maps before venturing out of the house. My father's preference was not to look at a map at all and just, as he would say over and again, follow his nose.

Sometimes I read books that fail as books but succeed as little masterclasses in the writer's inner nature. Sometimes I'll read what seems like good story but realize, to my disappointment, that I have learned nothing of any consequence about the writer. The best books do both. When I read Patrick Radden Keefe's *Empire of Pain*, his brilliant account of the Sackler family and the painkiller Oxycontin, I think I spent nearly as much time on the endnotes as I did on the main text itself. The book is built on a staggering amount of original research: hundreds of interviews, thousands of pages of documents. The endnotes *are* the point! Because the one thing the reader keeps asking himself – this reader, anyway – is: how did Keefe do it? Who is this person capable of uncovering a story that the Sacklers were so determined to keep quiet? There's a line in one of Keefe's endnotes about when he was reporting the part of the story that takes place in the 1940s and 1950s. He was racing around to talk to those few who remembered those years, to get to them before they died. Doesn't the image of Keefe, frantically running from one nursing home to the next, tell you everything you need to know about his ambition and urgency as a storyteller? In another point in the endnotes, he says he relied heavily on the privately published memoirs of the ex-wife of Arthur Sackler, the family's patriarch. Only twelve copies of the memoirs were ever printed, Keefe tells us. Naturally I went online immediately and tried to find one for myself. No dice. I am not Patrick Radden Keefe.

Earlier in my career, I used to be free with my advice to other writers. I once went to a journalism conference and gave a stern address about how to exactly do this or not. I look back on that lecture today with embarrassment. What I should have done was to describe what I do, as simply as I could. And then said: 'This does not mean you should do the same. I am telling you what I do because I want you to understand who I am. And in your own writing, you should look to do the same, to make something that reflects what you care about and how you like to see the world. That is one of the ways writers give pleasure to the people who read their words. The reader hears a story. And, at the same time, the reader gets to know someone new.

John Gray

author of *Feline Philosophy*

In *Thoughts for the Times on War and Death* (1915), Sigmund Freud wrote, 'In the realm of fiction we discover that plurality of lives for which we crave.' What Freud believed about fiction, I believe to be true of reading in general. It is often in non-fiction that we find the other lives we need to complement the one and only life we possess.

Freud was writing soon after the outbreak of the First World War. The expectation of steady progress that had animated European civilization in what came to be seen as a lost age of security had been overturned. This is often regarded as a time of disillusion. Freud described it as one that realized life is a game with no 'return match'. What he discerned in the Great War was the ineradicable element of fatality in human existence.

Our most important experiences are irreversible, Freud believed, shaping our lives into tangles that cannot be unravelled. Through psychoanalysis, we may be able to understand why we are as we have become. But no one who reads Freud can doubt that for him the goal was reconciliation with fate. As he understood it, psychoanalysis works insofar as it enables us to accept ourselves.

Reading is a different way of dealing with our fates. When we read, we are able to enter into lives that are unlike any that we can live. For a short spell we are free to inhabit another world, better or worse than our own but quite distinct from it. During the siege of Leningrad in 1941–4, the citizens of that heroic and tragic city read in order to escape mentally from the deadly trap in which the Nazis had sealed them. Among the books they read and loved, we know from diaries and memoirs, were Charles Dickens's *Great Expectations* and J. B. Priestley's *The Good Companions*. These books called up lives their readers had never known. In this worst of times, reading was more than an escape. For many, it was a defiant assertion of the joy of being alive.

Our time of lockdown is not comparable in severity, but its trials are for us real enough. We too want to escape confinement. The books we read may be biographies, such as Richard Zenith's *Pessoa: An Experimental Life*; memoirs, like Mary Gaitskill's *Lost Cat*; or a work of visionary science, like James Lovelock's *Novacene: The Coming Age of Hyperintelligence*. Each of them transports us outside of ourselves: into the mind of a singular genius, who lived himself in an imagined world; into the life of someone whose world was transformed by a one-eyed feline; and into the larger cosmos, poised on the brink of a new phase of evolution, of which we are a part. When reading books like these we transcend our time and place, shake off our all-too-familiar sense of self and enjoy a respite from fate.

Reading is many things, including one of life's most enduring pleasures. But above all, perhaps, reading is an exercise in freedom of mind, through which we can view the variety of the human scene and the vastness of what lies beyond.

Jonathan Haidt

author of *The Coddling of the American Mind*

THREE EMOTIONAL REASONS FOR READING

There are many reasons why people are willing to pay a little bit of money and a lot of scarce time for the privilege of moving their eyes across someone else's words. As a social psychologist who studies the emotions, I'll just mention three ideas I've encountered that help to illuminate my own joy in reading.

First, there is the psychological state known as 'narrative transportation', studied by Melanie Green at Ohio State University. It's the state of flow we get into as readers when the 'real world falls away' and the book seems to turn its own pages. So much of our lives is spent in the shallows – that haze of emails and texts and to-do lists. Great books bring us away from all that, and we feel refreshed afterwards.

Second, there's the emotion of 'moral elevation', first described (as far as I know) by Thomas Jefferson in 1771, in a letter in which he advised a younger man on what kinds of books he should acquire for his library. Along with a catalogue of serious and dignified titles in philosophy and history, Jefferson urged the inclusion of fiction, despite its association with the reading preferences of young women. The reason, he said, was that great writing can trigger uplifting and educational moral emotions:

> When any ... act of charity or of gratitude, for instance, is presented either to our sight or imagination, we are deeply impressed with its beauty and feel a strong desire in ourselves of doing charitable and grateful acts also. On the contrary, when we see or read of any atrocious deed, we are disgusted with its deformity, and conceive an abhorrence of vice.

Jefferson believed that well-written fiction is often more powerful than less skilfully portrayed non-fiction. He noted that beautiful prose can 'dilate [the reader's] breast and elevate his sentiments as much as any similar incident which real history can furnish'.

Third, there's the emotion of awe, that great white whale of emotions, one that I spent much of my younger life seeking. In a review of the literature on the subject that I wrote with my friend Dacher Keltner, we concluded that a wide variety of experiences count as awe as long as they have two features: 1) the perception of vastness, and 2) something in the experience that cannot be accommodated within one's current mental structures; those structures must be changed, expanded or rebuilt. We typically imagine awe experiences at the rim of the Grand Canyon, or at the foot of a revered musician or religious leader. But there's a subtype of awe, sometimes called epiphany, that can be given to us either by a great orator or by a great non-fiction writer who explains a portion of the universe to us. When I think about the small pantheon of books that I treat as sacred objects, it is because of my gratitude for the awe I experienced and the revised mental structures that I still carry with me, long after spending one or two dozen hours moving my eyes across that author's words.

Thomas Halliday

author of *Otherlands*

How many times have you seen a film or book proclaim that it is 'based on a true story'? There is undoubtedly a minor thrill in knowing that whatever is unfolding is – to a first approximation, at least – true. It used to be very fashionable for authors to blur the boundaries between reality and fiction in their novels – Victor Hugo does this in *Les Misérables* with the town of M_____-sur-M__, and Dostoevsky puts two in the opening sentence of *Crime and Punishment*. Redacting fictional characters and places brings an air of authenticity and authority, fiction disguised as fact.

Some, no doubt, read non-fiction with the simple aim of learning new facts. Few, however, would regularly sit for an evening or spend a long railway journey flicking through a textbook. Reference books, while dense in useful information, are usually not what we want as readers. What we want are stories, and we find those in abundance in the real world, just as we do in the invented tales of novelists.

Where fiction, however, is a mirror, reflecting the internal world of emotion and thought, non-fiction is a lens that looks outwards. It is a lens that directs us toward the rest of the world and magnifies that which the author wants to show. As such, it is always a vision of reality from the point of view of the author, informed by the author's relationship with reality. In works of scientific non-fiction, the reader sees the everyday world in a new light, having revealed facets of reality, whether physical or biological, that our experiences lack. Histories and books on politics and social issues bring fresh views from people all over the world and throughout time, from life experience that you as the reader will never have, and contain just as many tales of love, loss, conflict, achievement, misunderstanding and tragedy as a novel. A cookbook is a journey of new ideas, the potential of new sensory experiences. What non-fiction gives, more than anything else, is perspective. Finish a good non-fiction book, and you will see angles on reality you have never seen before, thrilling, wonderful, and provoking.

Sudhir Hazareesingh

author of *Black Spartacus*

THE HOME LIBRARY

I was initiated into reading in my father Kissoonsingh's library. He was a Mauritian writer, academic, politician and publisher, and I grew up on the island in the 1960s and 1970s surrounded by his books. Our family home in Phoenix had a large room designed as a library running across the top floor. The only other room up there was an enclosure for prayer; it was a floor dedicated, in effect, to things spiritual.

When I was a child, the library was a safe haven where I retreated from 'downstairs', the tumultuous adult world of visitors, meals, phone calls and urgent instructions shouted out to various staff. Very quickly I realized that this reading material could also provide an escape into remote and sometimes mysterious lands. One of my earliest of these great voyages was in a beautiful book called *Mao: Réalités d'une légende* (1976) by the Sinologist Emile Guikovaty. Guikovaty exposed me to the esoteric world of late Maoism, where all that was essential was expressed through symbols, complex codes and veiled allusions. I warmed to Maoism, its contempt for American and Soviet imperialism, and its solidarity with demands in the Global South for equality, liberation and sovereignty. Although my youthful flirtation with Maoism was brief, it left me with an enduring aversion to neo-colonialism in all its forms, and a fascination for charismatic leaders and revolutions.

Poetry was one of the literary genres my father particularly loved. It spoke to his free spirit, his admiration of beauty and his sense of creativity. He was attached to Shelley's quip about poets being 'the legislators of the universe', and a well-thumbed edition of Shakespeare's sonnets was always within reach. He published anthologies of Léoville L'Homme and Robert-Edward Hart, the most eminent Mauritian poets of the later nineteenth and early twentieth centuries, and also corresponded actively with figures such as T. S. Eliot and Rabindranath Tagore; their responses carefully preserved, some even displayed (I remember a signed print of *Krishnakali* hanging in the living room). The second half of the twentieth century witnessed the great wave of anti-colonial struggles, and my father was close to the Mauritian poets who supported our fight for independence from British rule, such as Malcolm de Chazal and Marcel Cabon. I became fascinated by Chazal's defiance of convention (he was influenced by French surrealism) and Cabon's embrace of all the constituent components of Mauritian culture – African, Asian, European.

Among my father's most cherished acquaintances was the Senegalese president Léopold Sédar Senghor, one of the pioneers, alongside Aimé Césaire, of the *négritude* movement; I can still picture him in animated conversation with my father in our library. Among the subjects of discussion was history: how it shaped who we were, but also how its dominant European narratives could distort and even erase our past. My father believed that Mauritians would never be fully free unless we recovered the roots of our heritage, brutally severed by the experiences of colonialism. This belief resonated with me then and even more so now that I have gained a better understanding of how the past can be actively erased. The library was also a repository of primary sources: official colonial reports, pamphlets, diaries and memoirs, newspapers and magazines from Europe, Africa, Asia; these materials mostly spilled on to the floor and rose in stacks in corners. I have no doubt where my passion for archival research was born.

The two passions of my older brother Sandip were Russian literature and the Napoleonic Wars. He seemed to know every intimate detail of the imperial epic, from Marengo to Waterloo, so it was through him that I was introduced to many of the classics of Napoleonic literature, such as Marcel Dunan's erudite edition of the *Mémorial de Sainte-Hélène*. French revolutionary history also trickled into our everyday life. Sandip would bestow the name of a

Napoleonic marshal upon each family member, while officials who seconded my father in his various tasks were nicknamed either Duroc or Bertrand, after Bonaparte's efficient *grand-maréchaux du palais*. Any dodgy Englishman we came across was of course named Hudson Lowe, the Emperor's jailer at Sainte-Hélène. These designations changed from time to time, depending on the ebb and flow of our extended household – except for my mother Thara, who firmly ruled everything at home: she always remained the Emperor. Novels were about life, but life, as Napoleon had famously said of his own existence, could be a novel too.

Peter Hennessy
author of *A Duty of Care*

Curiosity, literacy and memory are what distinguishes our species from all others. Reading is the supreme activity that replenishes all three – the greatest accumulator of human capital.

It also slakes our craving for both the individual and the collective. When we apply eyes and mind to the page, it is a moment of solo enrichment that simultaneously plugs us into a shared world. Anyone, if they wish, can read that same page provided it is published in their language. It is not a zero-sum activity. Our absorption, our pleasure and our stimulation do not diminish anyone else's enjoyment.

If we are lucky, we never lose what Albert Einstein called 'a holy curiosity', and life itself is a constant page-turner – an unceasing oratorio with reading as its recitative.

Scott Hershovitz

author of *Nasty, Brutish, and Short*

'Reading is a superpower,' I told my kids when they were trying to learn.

Rex bought it. The idea that squiggly lines contained stories struck him as magical. And it was hard. He felt like he was being trained in an ancient art. But his younger brother, Hank, would have none of it.

'It's not a real superpower,' he said.

'What's a real superpower?' I asked.

'Flying.'

'Are you kidding? Flying sucks,' I said.

'Why?'

'It's cold up there. You get bugs in your teeth. And your hair looks crazy when you land.' The real hero of *Superman* is the product that keeps his curl in place.

'Yeah, but if you can fly, you can go anywhere you want,' Hank said.

'No, you can't.'

'Yes, you can.'

'Can you fly to the past?' I asked.

'No,' Hank said.

'Can you fly to the future?'

'No, but you can fly anywhere *now*,' Hank said.

'Can you go see Superman?' I asked.

'No,' he said. 'Superman's not real.'

'Hank, if you can read, you can go to the past. You can go to the future. And you can even go see Superman.'

'I can't talk to him,' he said.

'No, but he can talk to you – if you can read.'

'Sort of,' he said, which I took as a win. Hank never gives more than grudging acceptance.

But years later, he agrees: reading is a superpower. And now, it's *his* superpower. It takes him anywhere he wants to go. He loves graphic novels about Greek gods. He loves fantasy worlds filled with fantastic creatures. And when he has a question – about almost anything – he can look up the answer himself.

At night, the boys and I read together. Before they came along, I thought I'd left fantasy worlds behind. I love a good mystery novel and often take one on a trip. But mostly, I read to learn about the world I live in.

I'm drawn to books that render arcane aspects of it accessible: Helen Czerski's *Storm in a Teacup* (which makes physics so simple I read it to Rex); Witold Rybczynski's *Last Harvest* (which explains why we live in houses and are stuck with suburban sprawl); and James McManus's *Positively Fifth Street* (an introduction to the world of high-stakes poker, with a murder mystery to boot).

I love to read philosophy, too. Which makes sense; I'm a philosopher. I love to think through a puzzle with an author on a page.

But reading with the boys has reignited my love for fiction. Rex even has me reading comic books again – for the first time since I was fifteen.

We snuggle in bed with Batman. We like him best, since he doesn't have any superpowers (save reading). But we also debate which superpower would be best if you could only have one. (Even comic books provide fodder for philosophical reflection.)

I asked Hank recently. 'Which is better: reading or flying?'

'I don't know. They're both pretty cool,' he said.

'If you had to pick, which would you want?'

'That's really hard,' he said. 'Flying would be fun. But to do stuff, you need to be able to read. And I like stories a lot.'

'So what would you pick?'

'Both.'

'Nope, you've got to choose.'

'I can't,' he said. 'Can you ask me an easier one?'

'Okay. Would you rather be able to read or fart so strong you could blow buildings down?'

'That's a supervillain power!' he said between giggles. 'I wanna read.'

So that's our family pitch for reading: it's better than farting, and maybe as good as flying.

Rosemary Hill

author of *Time's Witness*

To study the past is to travel in time. As the antiquary Charles Stothard wrote in a letter to a friend, by exploring history 'we live in other ages than our own'. Living only in one time, like living only in one place, limits the view. Stothard was twenty-five, and he was making an excursion to Kent in the summer of 1811. One day, finding himself at the Roman fort of Regulbium, he decided to do some beachcombing before dinner. Along the strand he picked up Roman bricks and tiles, a brass ring with a fragment of carved glass in it, and some coins. Looking up at the cliffs he noticed skeletons, clearly visible, lying in strata, and speculated that these were early Christian burials. As I read his letters I find that, while he is trying to understand the early English past, I am standing next to him on the Saxon shore near Herne Bay, marvelling at the Georgian landscape littered with such spectacular finds. Yet in Stothard's day these remains were interesting only to antiquaries, the pioneers whose investigations mark the beginning of modern archaeology.

Important as he is to the history of antiquarianism, Charles was never famous. His letters were meant for his friends and family, which makes them all the more enjoyable to read. It is in the private lives of more-or-less ordinary people that we find the texture of the past, the food, the furniture, the everyday. In these letters the great events of history, the French Revolution, the Napoleonic Wars, are in the background, which is how most of us experience them. Reading the letters of people not unlike myself I become involved with them. To anyone who finds human character, individual motives and emotions interesting, private correspondence is fascinating. When it stretches over years it becomes compelling. As I read on, I watch friendships develop and marriages break down. I follow the outcome of quarrels, see how hopes or ambitions are realized or fail, and all with the godlike vision of posterity. I know the answers. Will she say 'Yes'? Will the baby be a boy? Is this illness serious? I have more than once found myself in tears over the sorrows of writers long-since dead – and laughed aloud at family jokes made a century before I was born. Young Stothard's letters from Kent are poignant to me, because, while I admire his intellectual originality, I know that he will die young leaving a desolate, pregnant wife.

Today, Regulbium, near Reculver, has been written up and tidied up. Nearby Richborough, where Stothard wandered alone and was 'agreeably surprised' to find a more substantial ruin than he had expected, now belongs to English Heritage, who describe it as 'perhaps the most symbolically important of all Roman sites in Britain'. The urns and fragments of statuary that once lay unregarded on the sand are safe in glass cases, and this of course is a good thing. Yet I envy Stothard and his sense of discovery. I also take note that our veneration for what we now call 'heritage' is not of so very long standing, and it is not to be taken for granted. By reading I see where I stand in time, how I got here and how the past casts a light into the future.

Clare Jackson
author of *Devil-Land*

Why are biographies always included as literary stowaways in my holiday packing? Well, a key prerequisite for any historian is insatiable curiosity, and, in this regard, biographies are satisfyingly nutritious. And nostalgically remembering past holidays prompts recollections of what I read on those vacations. Under shady pines at a Finisterre *gîte* one August, I relived sixteenth-century France's bloody religious wars through Sarah Bakewell's imaginative biography of Michel de Montaigne, *How to Live*. Another year, abstaining from a day's pony-trekking in Guardalavaca when pregnant, I substituted stifling Cuban humidity for Antarctic blizzards, absorbed by David Crane's *Scott of the Antarctic*. Sometimes, of course, uninvited literary companions may arrive in others' luggage. There was once what felt like three of us enjoying a bakingly hot week in a comfortable Puglian farmstead, as my husband retreated daily behind Sheridan Gilley's monumental *Newman and His Age*. And Newman's was a long life: appointed as a cardinal aged seventy-eight, he lived another eleven years – in Gilley's words, elevated 'in his countrymen's imagination in a remote blaze of sacred purple glory, and as a gilded joss-stick in the exotic temple of late Victorian Catholicism'.

For as much as I love reading fiction, it's the biographical details that lodge themselves in my mind. Whenever I enter a voting booth, for example, I recall Virginia Woolf's shock when her cook, Nellie Boxall, anticipated a Labour victory in the 1929 election by predicting 'we are winning'; as Alison Light gently admonishes, in *Mrs Woolf and the Servants*, it hadn't occurred to Woolf 'that there might be a common political cause between mistress and maid'. As 'history made flesh', biography bridges external structure and personal agency. Family circumstance, social background and world events condition all lives to some extent, but individuals make wise or foolish decisions, pursue careers and form relationships, helped and hindered by serendipitous chance and the odd crossed wire. Sticking with the psephological theme, Adam Sisman's biography of Hugh Trevor-Roper describes how the historian and his wife, Xandra, drove from Oxford to the Scottish Borders purposely to vote in the Roxburgh, Selkirk and Peebles by-election in 1965, won by the young Liberal candidate, David Steel. But having cast their votes, Xandra was 'both amazed and horrified' to discover that her husband had voted for Steel, rather than the Conservative candidate, Robin McEwen, who was a family friend; 'they had driven all the way to Scotland to vote, but their votes had cancelled each other out'. In myriad ways, from what W. B. Yeats once described as 'the bundle of action and incoherence that sits down to breakfast', biographical subjects are rendered – with differing degrees of skill and sensitivity – into intelligible individuals whose inspiring, extraordinary and chaotic experiences vividly augment our own. And, for a child who grew up with a stalwart cadre of imaginary friends, stashing a new biography in my holiday baggage presents an irresistible opportunity to make the acquaintance of someone I've never met.

Jennifer Jacquet
author of *The Playbook*

OTHER MINDS

Most of what I read could be categorized as scientific papers, which are written in accordance with scientific norms – a manner that suggests there is no author, only scientific 'truth'. Philosopher Michael Strevens believes this rigorous exclusion of subjective experience, ideology and aesthetics from scientific writing is what allows science to proceed as if these social forces don't exist. This purposeful dulling of the senses permits us to deal with, to the greatest extent possible, the facts. The result is that when I read Robert Sapolsky's scientific papers, perfectly executed in terms of the prose, I can connect with his ideas. That is not the same as reading *A Primate's Memoir* and feeling connected to Sapolsky's mind.

At peak performance, a book allows one mind to connect with another. Some would surely argue that this can also be achieved through letters, movies, or a social media account. But the book remains my favourite form, with its singular, sustained voice stripped bare to language, without the manipulative powers of images or music.

Of course, not all books are the same. I find non-fiction can be superior to fiction in terms of revealing the author's mind. There is a thrilling, emergent property of genius from the essays of Ursula Le Guin, David Foster Wallace, Annie Dillard and Joan Didion that I simply don't get from their novels (surely my own failure, but that is the kind I am least able to escape).

I was never fortunate enough to meet Simon Gray, although having read his memoir *The Smoking Diaries* I would seek his advice based on his observations of Steven Seagal alone: '. . . his retro ponytail, his lushly muscled body with its hints of corpulence to come, his quick-footed, buttock-rolling walk, and above all the softly growling tone in which he issues warnings of death or castration'. The way this guy writes and what he sees makes me like his mind.

A book can fill me with respect. Naomi Klein's *No Logo* was prescient. Jane Mayer's *Dark Money* was fearless. If after 900-plus pages of Robert Proctor's eloquent and damning history of the cigarette manufacturers, *Golden Holocaust*, it is not evident that Proctor is a leader of the resistance, one must admit it's true after his final acknowledgement: 'Last but not least, I would like to thank those many cigarette industry lawyers with whom I have sparred over the past dozen-odd years . . . I am particularly grateful in this regard to [here he names fourteen individuals], all esquires for the tobacco trade.'

Being incisive or witty or brave is not enough for some people, though. Some writers want to really mess with us, and I, for one, enjoy being messed with. They are intent on dismantling or blurring familiar forms. Their ideas are meta, their jokes inside. They want us to use second order theory of mind. They want us to connect not only to their mind, but also to what they have read, and to what their mind did with what they read. It would be difficult to fully appreciate Hanya Yanagihara's fictional *The People in the Trees* without having read Colin Turnbull's non-fiction. Writers like Joy Williams, David Shields and Geoff Dyer seem to be asking: can you keep up? Sometimes I can. Or I believe that I can, and that makes life less lonely.

Lucy Jones
author of *Losing Eden*

It is bewildering, isn't it, to find oneself alive on the third rock from the sun? What are we doing here, on a ball of basalt that has been hurtling through the cosmos for more than four billion years? It is, for me, sometimes a baffling existence. And within that, what strange boxes we have made for ourselves! Bizarre systems and structures, interpretations and explanations, which can constrict and skew our realities.

Like others, I read first and foremost to make sense of the planet we inhabit, and the societies we have built upon it. I read to learn about slime moulds and space, and ambivalence and memory, and sentences and childhood and tardigrades. We read because we are, as a species, naturally curious: we crave information beyond that which we require to meet our basic needs of survival.

I read to know more about love and fear; about ethics, and aesthetics, and metaphysics; I read to become more literate in emotions and psychology. I read to laugh.

I read to soothe my children. I read to soothe myself. I read to enjoy cadence and metre; to fall asleep and to wake myself up. I read to show my children that, with a book in your hands, you can travel anywhere. Books are time machines made from trees: agents of transformation and illumination. They bestow new eyes on the world, again and again.

I read for 'cosmic insignificance therapy', to feel smaller in the face of galaxies. I read to shrink myself less, to swell in the face of patriarchy and capitalism. I read to peer beyond my anthropocentric and socio-cultural context and learn how others might think and feel; to simplify and to complicate my understanding of what on earth is going on.

In reading, we encounter texts that writers have written and rewritten, edited and distilled, held up to the light and questioned, weighed and examined; we experience one of the most lucid, malleable and thoughtful forms of communication. Through the moulding and sculpting and forging of small black letters – straight lines, dots, curves, flicks – we have built the world around us, and we can build it again.

The root of the word 'read' as it first appeared in the English language is the Old English word *rædan*, which meant, as well as the interpretation of written symbols, to discern the meaning of, chiefly, a dream or a riddle. For those of us perplexed by so much of life today, books help us to solve mysteries, answer questions and escape when it's all getting too much. Ultimately, they are a reminder of the miraculous absurdity of life on earth; a means of feeling less alone in this spectacular, precarious world.

Marit Kapla

author of *Osebol*

BOXING DAY AT NOON

It was Boxing Day at noon, and my nineteen-year-old daughter and I were emptying the dishwasher. I told her that I had tried to write that morning without success.

'It's supposed to be about why I read,' I told her. 'I just end up with the most basic stuff. I don't know. Why do you read?'

She handed me two clean glasses. I put one of them into the other and stowed them in the crammed cupboard above the sink without wiping off the remaining water. After a short silence she said, 'Whenever I read Ursula LeGuin, I feel honoured that her thoughts are running through my mind.'

She went to her room to collect LeGuin's novel *The Left Hand of Darkness*. Back in the kitchen, she started quoting from the author's introduction.

I told my daughter quite seriously that it would be better if she wrote my piece for me.

I had made several attempts in the past weeks to write about why I read. One night when I couldn't sleep, I had put the light on again, fetched my laptop and tried to remember exactly why I had read the books I had l read this year. I divided the books into two categories: 'work' and 'pleasure'. It turned out that I had read two thirds for work and one third in the pursuit of pleasure. But very often what had started out as a duty had become a source of enjoyment in itself: clearly, then, the two are not mutually exclusive. And things had not always gone to plan. Just as there were books that offered much more than expected, so too were there highly anticipated books that I never got around to finishing.

When I started reading the Danish poet Inger Christensen's

collection of essays *Del af labyrinten* (*Part of the Labyrinth*) in its Swedish translation by Marie Silkeberg, it was to prepare for a panel conversation. But the included poem 'Vandtrapper' ('Water-steps'), a composition about the fountains of Rome in which a few words and images repeat and dissolve until they begin to create new meanings, turned out to be an unforgettable, life-expanding experience. Immediately, I wanted to write a similar poem myself. It reminded me not only of the joy of writing but of the joy of existence in itself; of how strange life is – and how wonderful.

In 2012, when I read a review of the Belarusian Nobel Prize winner Svetlana Alexievich's *У войны не женское лицо* (*The Unwomanly Face of War*) in Kajsa Öberg Lindsten's Swedish translation, I went and bought the book mainly because I wanted to know more about how Soviet women fought in the Second World War. In part, also, I was intrigued as a journalist by Alexievich's technique of interviewing a lot of people on the same subject and then building her book from their words, like a chorus of voices. It was an impulsive purchase. Little did I know, as I first opened that book's pages back at home, what a great inspiration Svetlana Alexievich would go on to become in my own writing.

I came to think about our neighbours' daughter, who, long ago, as a babysitter to my sister and me, had first taught me to read. I see her sometimes when I am visiting Osebol, the village where I grew up. We chat a little as I buy food from her in the supermarket that is now run by the local football club. Every time, I think about how she once expanded my world.

By lunch on Boxing Day, I found I had written a poem of one line: 'I read because I can.'

I looked at my daughter, who, in order to crack the reading code, had once forced me to repeat every single letter in every word visible on signs, food packages and shopping bags. She was putting the cutlery in the top drawer.

'I should finally read *The Left Hand of Darkness*,' I said.

Alex Kerr

author of *Finding the Heart Sutra*

IN THE ATTIC

When I was fourteen, my family lived in a house in Alexandria, Virginia. Just outside my bedroom on the second floor, a string hung from the ceiling in the passageway. If you pulled on it, the ceiling opened up, and a stairway – a sort of ladder with steps – descended, and you could climb up to the attic. It had low triangular ceilings and was always oppressively hot. I was a classic misfit in school, with few friends, and not interested in sports and TV programmes – all the things my fellow students were engrossed in. I was into Japan (where we had recently lived) and, worse, Italian opera. So the attic became my gateway, my escape. I'd slip up into the quiet heat and pull the steps up behind me. From the passageway below you could only see the ceiling. Nobody knew I was up there.

My parents kept all the usual bric-a-brac in the attic, but among it all were shelves and shelves of books, which I read more or less at random. One of these was Oswald Spengler's *Decline of the West*. I ignored almost everything in this impenetrable work, which I could only barely understand. But I did manage to glean one cool insight: Spengler wrote that the mastery of harmony achieved in chamber music was the supreme glory of the West. After this, for the West, it was all downhill.

Another book which was to have a huge influence on my life was Marguerite Yourcenar's *Memoirs of Hadrian*. Again, I can remember but one vignette from that book, where Hadrian comments that the beautiful Antinous would become soft with inactivity, but, just a few days back in the hunt and his body would become firm again.

There was something even better up there than Spengler or Yourcenar. On those shelves were years and years of issues of the magazine

Galaxy Science Fiction, in which seminal works by Asimov, Heinlein and many others were serialized. There were other science fiction magazines whose names I've now forgotten, and what might have been a first edition of Ray Bradbury's *Fahrenheit 451*. Mopping the sweat off my forehead in the heat of that attic, I happily devoured these books, reading my favorites over and over again. I thrilled at the blend of philosophy and eroticism in ancient Rome, and I was equally swept away by the fantasy world of science fiction. My parents thought I was becoming weird and worried about me.

Now I'm approaching seventy, still weird, and I realize that the attic has never gone away. Reading is still a secret place where I'm all alone. Once I pull the stairs up behind me, the difficulties of the world downstairs disappear. I'm back in my hideaway, crouched beneath the low A-frame of the attic roof, wandering in alien worlds.

When I look back at what I read in those days, a unifying theme would be fantasy, as in *Galaxy Science Fiction* or Yourcenar's Rome. In college I was accused of having a taste for the exotic, of waving fantastical anecdotes around as if they were sparklers. Yet my reading in adulthood has largely not been in the fantasy vein, or novels at all – with the exception of Proust, whom I never stop revisiting. Most of my reading is non-fiction.

The question is, where are the sparklers to be found in factual writing, where the last thing a writer is supposed to do is to engage in leaps of the imagination?

Lately I've been consumed by the biographical essays of Lytton Strachey. He deftly captures the human essence of people who lived just a century or two ago, but whose lives now appear utterly foreign to us. Of Madame du Deffand, mistress of a brilliant circle in eighteenth-century Paris, he writes, 'Then at moments her wit crystallised; the cataract threw off a shower of radiant jewels, which one caught as one might.' But her salon was in decline: 'They had fallen into the yellow leaf.' In the end, we see the heartsick old society lady as she lies dying in the ruins of her charmed but lonely life. 'She died as she had lived – her room crowded with acquaintances and the sound of a conversation in her ears.' Madame du Deffand, before

Lytton Strachey took up her biography, was barely a historical foot-note. Strachey elevated her world into one of wicked delight and lingering pathos.

Much of my reading these days is highly practical – non-fiction books about topics I'm currently researching, such as forestry, one of Japan's modern disasters, or specialist volumes about Japanese art. In these books, the discoveries rarely arise from the finesse of the writer, but from a sort of treasure hunt. I'm an archaeologist on a mission. After enduring the endless hardship of sterile academic writing, and piling up mounds of useless curatorial mud, suddenly one golden artefact emerges.

I recently got curious about the early seventeenth-century high court noble Konoe Nobutada. He wrote a scratchy calligraphy more like a cranky Zen monk than a suave Kyoto aristocrat, and people have wondered how and why he created it. As I read, I found that, while Nobutada was born at the peak of a luxurious court, the Sho-guns of the time treated him shabbily; his life was one long string of failures, and then – a comment in an obscure journal – it turns out that he died of drink. An elegant prince, with an unsatisfying life, drowned in the end in alcohol – there's the key to Nobutada's inim-itable style. Like a tomb-digger of the old days, I revel in the fact that only I have found a prize that others had maybe also seen but had passed by. Imagine what Lytton Strachey could do with this.

As has been my habit since reading Spengler and Yourcenar as a teenager, I extract one gem, and forget most of the rest. I gather up my treasure and descend from the attic back to what used to be my bedroom and is now my office. The stairs swing back up into the ceiling. I've returned to the lower world of drudgery, but not empty-handed. Now it's time to start writing.

Ian Kershaw
author of *Roller-Coaster*

Interest: This is the most banal reason, but one that lies behind every impulse to read. Without an underlying interest in the subject matter, an inquisitiveness or curiosity about some thing or other, I would not be inclined to pick up a book in the first place.

Illumination: In the case of non-fiction especially I have the hope that my reading will enlighten me by casting new or further light on whatever issue has prompted my initial interest.

Inspiration: Works of non-fiction can offer as much mental stimulation as a novel or a moving piece of poetry or prose. Sometimes this can be profound. But there can also be inspiration on a lower level. If my own writing on a particular point has stalled, consulting relevant passages by a writer whom I admire (and whose judgement I trust) can inject the necessary ideas to get things moving again.

Imagination: Reading, not least, stirs the imaginative and creative powers. Unless, as can happen – especially with single-minded ideologues or other obsessives – it is simply to reinforce prejudice, we read to broaden our views, modify our outlook, or amend our thoughts by causing us to reflect in new or changed ways. The words on a page compel us to use our imagination. Over time, that can change our perspective on life.

Education: This is not just the obvious help that reading gives to the formal process of learning at school or university. Reading is a wonderful gift for life-long learning. I read to learn more about more, to educate myself further, to extend my knowledge. That is something that never ends.

Evaluation: I read also to evaluate the information I have accumulated. Non-fiction works frequently contain footnotes or endnotes that provide the references for a text. These are not a way of showing off how much one has read. Compiling them is actually tedious, but necessary. A bibliography at the end provides the information on the books used to underpin, reinforce and amplify what has been written. These works will have provided the author both with important information and also the necessary confirmation that what has been written is correct in the author's best judgement.

Relaxation: It seems less obvious to contemplate relaxing with a work of non-fiction than with a novel, or perhaps a crime-thriller. Like many others, I like detective stories – but I only read them to shut down for the day, managing a paragraph or two before I fall asleep each night (and quickly forget who committed the crime and why!). I do, however, read non-fiction for relaxation as well. My own work as a historian has concentrated for many years on some of the most disturbing aspects of modern history. So I relax by reading on other, far-distant themes, topics and eras, especially books on medieval or early-modern history. These give me pleasure – not the least of the reasons why I, and probably most other people, read.

Emma Jane Kirby
author of *The Optician of Lampedusa*

Once upon a time, I was a foreign correspondent and news journalist, and the overarching narrative of my life was witnessing and reporting other people's tragedies, wars and misery. For nearly three decades, my job was to report horrific events for an audience that hadn't been there to see it for themselves but which needed to know what had happened. I described events in the blunt, steely tone of fact, sanitizing little. Everything I wrote or broadcast seemed to be in an irrefutable tone of bold, block capitals.

So, after returning home from reporting plane crashes, migrant drownings or terror attacks, I simply could not face any more fact – or indeed any more ugly truths. Fearful of taking on board more worry, I'd filter out certain books on my shelves, rejecting all the non-fiction titles, be they about the horrors of running a field hospital in war-torn Syria, the fragility of the rural way of life in the Lake District or the struggle of trees to communicate and protect the weakest in their woodland social networks. I wanted to keep the world and its suffering at bay.

Instead, my refuge was in fiction, skulking with the menopausal, donut-craving Olive Kitteridge in sea-swept cafés in Crosby, Maine, or surfing shark-infested coves with Tim Winton's Pikelet in Western Australia, testing my nerve against the unrelenting forces of air and water. The works I chose were rarely happy-ever-after tales; I would still weep over Little Dorrit's fate in the Marshalsea debtors' prison, wake up in the night agonizing about Edith's choice at the end of Hotel du Lac, while pretty much every sentence in Toni Morrison's *Beloved* haunted me. Those novels felt real, and I feel I learned so much about life and human behaviour through reading them, but it was real life at one step removed, life kept at arms-length, life told almost in a different dialect. Choosing to read mainly fiction was about more than just being world-weary and needing escapism. It was also about escaping myself.

Lately, I have hung up my microphone and flak jacket and have begun story-lining and script-editing for a continuous drama. I am spending my days peopling a fictitious world with made-up villains and heroes and forcing them into myriad imagined jeopardies. But while living in a permanent state of disbelief is fantastic, I've also found it somewhat destabilizing, and it has had a curiously gravitational effect on my reading habits. Now, when I close my laptop for the day, I find I'm clutching at my non-fiction shelves to keep my sense of balance. I need (particularly during these crazy Covid times, in which nothing seems quite real) to anchor myself in solid fact, to root myself in reality. I hoover up history books, feast on the footnotes, graze the bibliographies for second helpings. Comfort comes from feeling the solid structure of the world around me, unfolding its blueprint and trying to figure out how it works – or at least how others perceive it works.

For me, the best non-fiction books are those that impart knowledge just as novels do: through the telling of stories. I love non-fiction authors who translate what might have been the turgid prose of a textbook into a poetic tale of astonishment. Just as I can be transported to the magical world of Hogwarts alongside Harry Potter, so I can find myself in another world of wonder reading Christopher de Hamel's *Meetings with Remarkable Manuscripts*, flitting through time and history alongside his 'migrating manuscripts', greedy for gilt. Likewise, Neil MacGregor's *A History of the World in 100 Objects*; while I enjoyed listening to his radio documentaries on the subject, reading his book gave me the space to flick back and forth through time at my own pace, forming my own connections to the objects and reflecting much more deeply on how humanity has shaped itself over the ages. Reading non-fiction challenges me to revise my opinions, but it also makes me feel connected. Michael Holroyd's biography of Augustus John painted such a complete picture of the flamboyant artist that I can no longer look at any of John's drawings and paintings without a genuine sense of missing the man, despite the fact he died almost a decade before I was born.

Good non-fiction not only hooks me into subjects I would have sworn I was not interested in, it teaches me far more than I bargain for when I skim the fly leaf. I may not have bought a goshawk chick after reading Helen MacDonald's *H is for Hawk* (although I will admit that shortly after finishing it I bought my first bird guide and my first bird feeder), but I did learn to confront my own grief as I read the astonishing account of her struggle to let go of her own tethered emotions while taming a bird of prey. Tramping the wild places of the Scottish Highlands with Christopher Nicholson and his *Among the Summer Snow* (while I sat on a long train journey), I still remember the moment when he found the last surviving patch of snow on the mountainside and when, squinting into the crystallized glare and beauty of it, I wept openly as I recognized my own mortality and the earth's fragility.

Non-fiction doesn't just inform us, it wakes us up, shakes our complacency, invites us to take a good and honest look at what's really out there. It takes us out of ourselves and then asks if we really just want to go back inside, now that we know what we know. Once you've read Raynor Wynn's *The Salt Path*, for example, you can't continue to pretend that you know nothing about homelessness. Once you've read Jeanette Winterson's moving memoir *Why Be Happy When You Can Be Normal*, you can't just block it out by curling up on the couch with a hot chocolate and re-reading *Oranges are Not the Only Fruit* in the hope it will just go away.

Just like a good novel, a decent non-fiction book helps us escape to other realms, countries and historical ages. But you can't undo knowledge. Once you know, you know - and there's simply no way back. But knowledge is power, of course, and that's why, for me, the true magic of non-fiction is that it always offers you the chance to find a way forward.

Ivan Krastev
author of *Is It Tomorrow Yet?*

Whenever I browse the non-fiction section in a bookshop, an analogy starts to haunt me. Isn't it true that we read memoirs, popular psychology, history and (usually apocalyptic) forecasts about climate change or about the state of our democracies for the same reason that British people voted for Brexit? Hoping to take back control of our lives – or at least our thoughts.

We read non-fiction books for the same reason Sherlock Holmes slowly focuses on every little detail, opens every drawer and goes through the rubbish bin while wandering around a crime scene. He looks for signs to help him uncover the mystery of the crime, hoping to find hidden traces that will bring valuable insights. But by spending hours reading pieces of half-burned letters or putting under his magnifying glass the ashes of a cigar, he also wants to signal to the outside world that he is a detective, someone who knows how to solve mysteries and who trusts in the power of the intellect to deal with uncertainty. The more the world in which we live looks to us like a crime scene, the more – in order to preserve our normality – we need to believe that we are detectives.

We read non-fiction books because we want the world to know that we feel intrigued and excited rather than threatened, overwhelmed or outraged by its complexity. We rely on them to unveil the world to us while letting other people know who we are.

Michael Lewis
author of *The Premonition*

I've always had friends who don't read much and who make persuasive cases for their way of life. Not very long ago an old friend told me with a kind of glee that he hasn't read a book since he graduated from college, forty years ago. And yet, in the intervening years, he'd only grown and prospered. He's built a successful business from scratch. He's been a model citizen. He has a happy family. And he's interested in, and interesting about, all sorts of things. Reading just isn't one of them.

People who think of themselves as readers tend to condescend to people who don't. But people who don't read can be equally condescending towards those who do. My friend is a good example. He thinks of me as a bit odd and a little naive about how the world actually works. If I were to put him in charge of improving my character, he might not start by slashing the amount of time that I was allowed to spend reading books. But he might.

I mention this because the sort of person reading this book probably just takes for granted the value of reading. Mostly I do, too. I've never thought of reading as having an opportunity cost, though clearly it does. I've never worried about what I may have missed while I was reading, or how my reading habits might somehow blind me to whatever is occurring in the world outside my reading material – though clearly they could do so. To explain why I read feels a bit like explaining why I eat. My motives are selfish. Like others, I read to escape the limits of my experience, to access the mind of some stranger, to learn about some new subject, and to fill empty time. I'm required to read a lot for work, but I'm at my best as a reader when the reading isn't required – which is to say that I am a better reader when I am not being paid to do it than when

I am. And I think a big reason that I get such joy from non-required reading is the feeling it has given me, since I was a little kid, surrounded by friends who didn't read all that much, of being let in on a secret. A part of the pleasure in any book still is in knowing that others will never discover it.

Daniel Lieberman
author of *Exercised*

Consider this: reading is a strange, modern behaviour that we never evolved to do. Of the 300,000 or so years in which our species has existed, humans started reading only about 5,000 years ago. That's barely 1 per cent of our existence. What is more, until the Industrial Revolution, just a handful of humans had the privilege of reading. From an evolutionary perspective, reading is nearly as novel and strange as driving cars or using credit cards.

The novelty of reading helps to explain why it's so hard to learn. Although reading these words may seem almost effortless, you had to train your brain slowly and arduously over many years to master this unnatural skill by coordinating a series of adaptations that evolved for other purposes. To read, your eyes first absorb the photons bouncing off a sequence of arbitrary symbols. Cells in the back of your eye transform that information into millions of electrical and chemical signals, which are transported to a specialized region in your brain, the occipital cortex. There, yet more electrical and chemical signals turn these lines and dots into a sort of dynamic map. That information then zips nearly instantaneously to multiple other parts of your brain that, together, reconstruct the signals into the sequence of words, making you consciously aware of precisely what I have written. Once your brain learns how to accomplish and integrate these many processes, then almost by magic you can resurrect whatever I or any other writer wished to convey.

Reading may be a remarkable, modern behaviour that, once mastered, conveys information efficiently and effectively, but I think an evolutionary perspective provides another compelling explanation for why we read. Consider that we evolved to be highly social creatures who cooperate by sharing not just food and affection but also ideas, emotions and knowledge. For millions of years, we communicated primarily by gesturing and talking. But when we learn to read, we open up another potentially deeper way of communicating that was unavailable to our pre-literate ancestors that literally lets others into our minds.

Compare listening and reading. If you were to read these words to me, my brain would perform a series of tasks to make sense of them. But they would be your words in your voice. If, however, I read the same words, my brain has to do some critical extra steps to re-create them before making sense of them. Whether I subvocalize them or not, your words and your thoughts also become my words and my thoughts. Consequently, when I read – especially well-crafted words about ideas or feelings – I sometimes feel like I have let another person into my mind. Our brains are somehow connected more deeply than through conversation. This intense connection also happens when we dance together, listen to music, or focus on a painting, but reading isn't just sensory, it's also intellectual. Right now, you are re-creating my thoughts in a profoundly intimate fashion as thoughts in your brain. Further, it doesn't matter when and where I wrote these words. For all you know, I wrote these words decades ago on a different continent.

The first scribes who scribbled for a tiny audience of other scribes would no doubt be astounded by today's world of publishing, nearly universal literacy, and the internet. Today we think it normal that millions of people in every corner of the globe can read and thus experience the same thoughts and ideas. But for all its apparent normality, let's celebrate that reading is an odd, amazing and utterly novel behaviour. That, too, is a pretty good reason to read.

Kate Manne
author of *Entitled*

'I write so I know I'm not crazy.' So wrote Charles R. Lawrence III, in introducing his tour de force of critical race theory, 'Unconscious Racism Revisited' (2008). In that piece, he confessed that he 'wrote to keep from going crazy, to explain to myself and others why the legal analysis of race that my professors, and later my colleagues, presented as wise and just often struck me as foolish and evil. And, I wrote with the hope that in my own struggle to understand what was making me crazy I might help all of us understand the insanity of white supremacy.'

I read for a similar reason – to understand the madness of misogyny, in particular. I read to try to undo the cultural gaslighting that I believe is a prevalent force for us all, mired as we are in white supremacy, patriarchy, ableism, classism, transphobia, homophobia and fatphobia. In reading the work of Rebecca Solnit, I manage to locate words to understand the bitter, frustrating experience of being condescended to by a man who assumes he knows more than I do about some subject in which I am expert. In reading the work of Sabrina Strings, I find a new and fascinating explanation for the origins of fatphobia in the racist derogation of the Black female body in the eighteenth century. In reading the work of Roxane Gay, I am able to crystallize my inchoate sense that there is a deep connection between sexual trauma and hunger of a kind that cannot be sated.

And I write to try to make a small contribution to the vast feminist and anti-racist effort to undo the collective gaslighting that stops us from not only saying, but seeing, what we are up against. Otherwise, we may well feel guilty as well as crazy for simply stating what is happening, or how the world needs to change going forward. But it is, and it must do.

Catherine Merridale
author of *Lenin on the Train*

The answer's simple at this time of year, December. Please take a look around my study and see all the piles of paperwork. Apart from the familiar reminder from Her Majesty's Revenue and Customs, there's a vast gas bill, a shopping list and two stapled pages from a nice man at the BBC. There's someone's grant proposal, too, and part of someone else's book. I know it's shameful, but the deeper strata surely continue down through several months. Why do we read? In my case, now? That's easy: to get away.

Pick up a book, a new one that still smells of print and paper, like expensive tea, and you can find instant relief from the noise of real life. It's like a conversation, too, but without all the boring parts. The author won't repeat herself, nor ramble on and reminisce, because she will have scrubbed away at every word till her text gleams. Most books are more involving, better organized and far more fluent than their authors ever were; they make more cogent arguments and most of them set out to please. What's more, if they should start to pall they're easy to shut up. So read on – it's not an exam – and find considered thoughts about the worlds, the lives and the ideas that someone else could not resist. With books, you can follow the course of the Amur, explore the pleasures of cosmology or simply peer into a liverwort, and all the time there is that warmth, the author's finest writing voice.

Most reading can be an escape, but non-fiction is more than that. It's also much more than a narrative of useful facts (if you can stand the sensation of being prodded all over by miniature pitchforks, the internet is fine for those). No, there is something magical, something both generous and personal, about the things that we discover through the pages of a book. It's entirely for us, we take our time, we understand at last. Read how a scientist from the Potawatomi

Nation sees our planet or take another look at the effects of war or even (if you must) the mechanisms of market economics. I'll read it all, I can't resist, but though it starts out as escape there's one more thing, and it's a most unbookish sort of gift. When I come back to this world, tax return notwithstanding, I'll come back more alive.

Rana Mitter

author of *China's Good War*

My academic work is in the field of Chinese history. One of the reasons I read that subject, as well as writing it, is the obvious reason: to learn more about the past experience of a fascinating country of global significance.

But there's another reason to read that working on China makes more apparent. In the west, we tend to assume that because something has been recorded, it will stay recorded. Yet in China, there is no guarantee that that is the case.

Censorship has been used by all Chinese regimes, but in the past decade or two, many books that have recorded problematic aspects of the past have appeared, then disappeared from the shelves in China. The era of digital books has made it much easier to read work from, and about, China at the press of a button. But it has also allowed censors in Beijing to remove, without notice or justification, books and articles on topics such as the coercive tactics of the Chinese Communist party or the actions of leaders now regarded as *personae non gratae*, such as the reformist Party leader Zhao Ziyang, who was placed under permanent house arrest in 1989. An e-book does not need to be burned. It can just be deleted.

So historians like me read about China for several reasons. We read to learn more about this great society and culture. We read to acknowledge that, for many sensitive topics, western readers have a privilege of reading material that is not available within China itself. But, increasingly, we read because we want to gather knowledge and make judgements while material is available to us, at a time when new technologies make it easier both to inform us, and to deny us knowledge. We read in the hope that the book or e-book will be there the next time we look for it, but fearful that it may not be.

George Monbiot

author of *Regenesis*

I read because I trust nothing else. Writing, or so I like to believe, is the medium in which claims are easiest to verify or to disprove. Of course, I also read because I love it. But in a world of bullshit, we need above all to determine where we stand.

I believe we should all strive to see both the beauty and the truth but, in doing so, to recognize that they are not the same thing. Some of the most beautiful passages in the English language (including Keats's famous axiom, 'Beauty is truth, truth beauty') reveal mistaken or confused ideas, while startling scientific revelations might be expressed in language that is as jarring as it is difficult, and might expose realities that are ugly and hard to accept.

Moreover, what 'makes sense' – in other words, what appeals to our intuition, and so seems beautiful – often bears no relationship to reality. Our narrative sense encourages us to interpret the world in linear and simple terms: cause and effect, time and distance, incidence and reflection. But this apprehension of the physical world, essential as it is, does not equip us to understand the way that complex systems work, whose properties often appear to defy common sense.

Our lives are entirely dependent on complex systems: living systems, atmospheric systems, oceanic systems, human society and the many subsystems (food supply, finance, politics, civic life) it has generated, the human body, the human brain. There is great beauty to be found in complexity, once you have begun to glimpse some of the ways in which these systems work. But it is a different beauty from the one we seek in the simple stories with which we navigate the world.

I believe that the reader's highest aspiration should be to travel freely through these spheres: the many spheres of beauty and the many spheres of truth.

Timothy Morton

author of *Being Ecological*

Governments want to tell you that 'science, technology, engineering, maths' (STEM) are the most important subjects. But reading is the real stem. Understanding what a fact is means understanding how to read. A fact is an interpretation of data: a reading. Yet these interpretations are based on all kinds of facts that are themselves interpretations. Up until recently, there were doors with MEN on them and doors with WOMEN on them. That was a fact, based on facts. Now more of us are accepting what the data means – how there are trans and intersex people who might not want to go through a door with MEN or with WOMEN on it.

We read based on facts. Facts are things that have been made (Latin, *facere*). Facts are made out of data, which are things that have been given (Latin, *dare*). Data isn't just scientific measurements. Data is, *This reminds me of my grandmother, That smells of cinnamon.* Poems and essays are data, waiting for you to interpret them. To *read* them. Whenever you read, you're interpreting, the same way a conductor interprets a musical score. Facts and data are from the past. They *are* the past. We aren't stuck in the past, just like we aren't stuck with a door with MEN written on it.

Facts are based on reading: *This is a towel.* I bet someone pointed to one and said 'towel' to you often enough when you were little so that you ended up 'knowing' that it was a towel. But, really, you were just reading. And so were they. *Towel* is a little token, a convenience, something from the past, like a pair of socks. You want to go for a walk, so you find your socks. You want to teach your child about towels, so you say *towel*.

Logic and maths are both kinds of reading. Logic is gathering stuff, 'reading' them like using the word *towel*. Maths is communing with stuff (sadly, STEM 'maths' is more like folding the laundry than communing). I know which is more important. It's maths. You wear clothes, then you wash and fold them. In a world where super-fast algorithms gather stuff about us all the time and sell that stuff to big corporations and politicians, I dare say we could do with a bit less gathering and some more communing. Just looking at something without needing to know what it is. The kind of thing mathematicians do. The kind of thing that you do when you read a poem. The kind of thing you don't do when you see the word *towel* in a department store.

You sometimes read because you want to be surprised. That doesn't mean that you want the surprises or you think they're a good idea. When you decide not to buy those dumplings at the airport but, instead, this book about dinosaurs or dating, you are signing up to be surprised. If you're parting with your hard-earned cash, you don't want to read something you already know. You want to finish a sentence, a chapter, a book, in a different place from where you started.

Reader, I married him. Isn't that one of the most powerful sentences in English literature? It bursts that realism bubble for a start. It's honest. It's very touching. You may have 'read' it a thousand times without actually reading *Jane Eyre*. So in a way you've already started to read *Jane Eyre*. Reading is so much more than just looking at the marks on the page and ... what are you doing when you do that? You're orchestrating a score. You're performing. You're doing a little ballet in your 'body' or your 'mind'.

When I put quotation marks around a word, I'm asking you to do some reading. I'm implying I find those binaries a bit suspect. I'm asking you to think that the word is overhearing itself, as if someone else was saying it. You stretch your mind – I'm using the word vaguely here – into the past, into uncertainty. Have you heard this word before, where, how? You stretch your mind into the future – what could Timothy Morton mean with these quotation marks?

Reading is really about the future. About the future as such, the future as something we cannot yet predict. The predictable future is just the past with a few more planks of pastness you're adding to it, nailing them together out over the abyss. Right now, this moment, this time of ecological crisis, the most important thing is to turn into good readers, namely, beings who are OK with being surprised by something they didn't expect. Beings who are OK with the future being different.

Reading a story is, at the very least, great practice for such a thing.

But isn't reading even bigger than that? Isn't reading also a very good image for how we do anything? Imagine being in a band: string quartet, small orchestra, black metal outfit ... You're listening to the other players. You're listening to your instrument. You're 'listening' to your musical heritage, attending to it. You're listening to the music itself. All these words like *listening* and *attending to* are synonyms for reading. Free will is overrated. Brain science tells us that by the time we have intended to do something, we're already doing it. Free will is actually a very toxic idea, along with words such as *subject*, *soul*, *mind* ... Words like that imply some kind of slave, or slavish material, something external we can manipulate with our will or mind or subjectivity. How we get rid of these words can also be toxic. If you get rid of 'subjects' only to say that the whole world is really just machinery, there's still a whiff of *subject* in the air. You've just said that the whole world is manipulable stuff. That screaming noise the lifeform is making as you insert a knife into it, that's just a mechanical sound. Don't worry. Cruelty is just a subjective illusion.

The idea of reading takes you quickly to the idea that you're not the only show in town. Machines read things. Alan Turing showed how they could. Do stones read as they tumble around the beach? If a machine head is reading a cassette tape – if my eyes are reading this essay – then isn't it also the case that stones are reading one another as they clatter and stumble in the swirling foam? The chameleon reads the surface they are resting on. Shakespeare could read humans so well that John Keats called him the *chameleon poet*.

If we want to grow up from words such as *subject* and *mind*, if we want to grow up into a world of science that cares for the biosphere we are a part of, we are going to need to lay these words to rest very, very carefully. We're going to need to read. You know what that Blue Marble image of Earth from space is saying? *Do you read me? Come in. Do you read?*

Jan-Werner Müller
author of *Democracy Rules*

Academics can be ruthless readers. They don't just use books; they plunder them, or they even rip them apart intellectually. They read instrumentally, driven by questions such as: is there an idea here that can help me build my argument? Information I need? This isn't about plagiarism – of course, the sources of ideas and information are acknowledged – but it *is* about more often than not failing to respect a work as a whole, as something that necessarily has to be read cover to cover, and as something that might have aesthetic integrity as a distinctive whole.

Academics must be ruthless readers. That's what some of us at least teach our students. Learn, we instruct them, how to ignore the padding, the summaries of existing debates to which an author might or might not just add a minuscule amendment. Or, for that matter, learn *not* to read the anecdotes that are put in to adorn books of history and politics which may or may not in the end have much of a real argument on offer. That art of *not* reading is a professional skill of sorts. (But then again: we might also teach them precisely how to do the padding, telling our students how to place their arguments inside an existing debate, making what they offer instantly recognizable to scholars and possibly a wider audience.)

And then there are the moments when one can't help oneself, when instrumental reading ceases, and a certain relentless professionalism just breaks down – and that's a good thing, too. It might have to do with an author's sensibility: we'll read Tony Judt's collected reviews long after the books on which he was commenting are forgotten; we'll read Heinrich Heine's journalism about politics in nineteenth-century Paris even when we have much more reliable historical accounts. Often enough, a philosophical text uncompromisingly demands close and comprehensive readings; here taking shortcuts would precisely be unprofessional – and unwise in a larger sense. And then there are the works with such aesthetic integrity that one cannot help but read them cover to cover, works you simply don't get if you rip them apart.

Veronica O'Keane
author of *The Rag and Bone Shop*

The brain never stops working to 'fit' whatever flows from the outside world through the senses to the neural maps of memory. The world 'out there' essentially gets converted to a maze of connected neurons in the brain. It is the way the neurons connect, the patterns of the webs of connection among neurons, that forms our individual ways of making sense, as well as a shared view of 'common' sense with others.

When a junior doctor in Dublin during the late 1980s I would steal away on late afternoons, hospital chaos allowing, to the small basement library. Those were the pre-internet days, when you would have to search for books and papers in libraries. Journals would be bound annually into hard-backed volumes, catalogued, and you'd follow the alphabet through the book isles to the journal title, then scan the year until you arrived at the one you were searching for, and with a sense of excitement lever the spine downwards. I would often linger until the last moment of closing, listening with one ear as the librarian walked to the light switch to lock up. If we did not have the journal, she would send my request card to the main library on the university campus, and sometimes we would have to source it from international libraries, meaning that I would have to wait for days to get the paper. The papers were precious clues in the treasure hunt to make sense of my research findings for my PhD, and expanded my searches to bigger questions in the emerging science of the brain. I was never happier than when lost in this chase.

Only reading can provide this kind of brain satisfaction. Of course one can now do in minutes on a smartphone what took me months back then. But this is not reading, it is information gathering, and the information does not have to 'fit' any mental model. It can hang alone as superficial as a forgotten piece of Christmas tinsel on a picture frame in January. Quick information provided by internet searches is not learning: it is only a loose bundle of possible truths. The corollary is picking up a non-fiction book with the reassurance that whatever you will read is written by someone who has long followed and pondered the subject matter and brings it to you as a trusted companion. Reading a book is a unique way of learning because it allows time to pause and consider, to match the new information to what you know. The reader sets the pace. Processing of information is so individual because we all know different things, have different areas of expertise and different abilities to process different types of information. Reading allows for this immense variability. One of the most enjoyable aspects of reading a book is being stopped by a sentence, one that you immediately re-read, and then re-read again, and again. You may be arrested by the beauty of the writing, or you may have an intuitive sense that it is true but as yet beyond your grasp. The sentence may linger hungrily for a few more chapters, driving you forward, until you arrive at the 'ah-ha' moment.

Perhaps one of the most thrilling aspects of reading is the possibility of opening up new ways of seeing and understanding, and in this, for me, science leads the way. My first journey into physics began with reading Stephen Hawking's *A Brief History of Time*. I found that I could not read more than a chapter at a time, not because I couldn't understand the language or that I got lost in the ideas, but because I knew that if I didn't allow the concepts to percolate slowly that it would somehow pass me by. On the surface it seemed self-evident, and I had a good grasp of the other sciences. I had had the same experience when I learned chemistry in school: the concepts were way bigger than the information. Reading Hawking was not augmenting or disrupting pre-existing neural patterns, it was creating novel neural assemblies. I understood immediately that wavelengths got shorter the further away they went, and that shorter wavelengths are a different colour, but the full impact only began to dawn on me years later. Fundamentally human perception (*seeing* the wavelengths as being different colours) is inseparable from the objective measures of physics (*distance* from earth as measured in time). Carlo Rovelli's beautiful book *The Order of Time* more recently taught me how measures of time cannot be separated from the human brain, from memory. His latest book, *Helgoland*, explores further the inseparability of neuroscience and physics, and the relativity of everything and everybody. Academia is complex, but presenting it in an accessible way forces the writer to draw the reader in through more general pathways of knowledge. In the same way that Carlo Rovelli has found his way to neuroscience, in my exploration of memory I have found my way to physics. In a sense, when we are looking at ways of measuring the world – physics – we are looking at how the brain measures and therefore understands. How would it be possible to communicate these concepts outside the immersion of writer and reader?

Reading a non-fiction book provides a unique way of analysing and bringing coherence to our internal models of the world. The more aware we are of this process, the more alive we are and the more connected we are to the flow of history, to the mysteries of the big unknowns and to the ever-moving science of life as it shifts from unknowns to new knowns, only to be disrupted or refined by new mysteries that have opened up from the new knowns. To share in these shifts to new and finer models of understanding the world is both to be connected to others, to the external human world of organic ideas, and to be connected to the happy experience of flourishing in our world of wonder.

Helen Parr
author of *Our Boys*

I swiped my card and walked into the library at the university in the West Midlands where I work. It was warm, and it was quiet. I climbed the stairs and went into the silent study area. Nobody looked at me. The students at their desks were working, heads down, books open, some with headphones, bottles of water in front of them. I went into the bookshelves and began to look.

It was at least eighteen months since I had been in the library. During the pandemic it had been shut, and one had to order books online and a librarian fetched them for you and left them at the front desk. There had been no browsing. There had been no immersion. There had been no connection, to all the other people, engaged in solitary work but in one place filled with books and dedicated to silence.

The feeling I had when I walked in startled me. I did not know that I had missed it. So many years, when I was 18, 19, 20, 21, right up until my 30s, when the children were born, were spent in libraries or in archives; reading and working alone, but always with the feeling that I – and all the others – were supposed to be reading, were supposed to be concentrating, were supposed to be studying, were trying to become scholars or, at least, scholarly. Reading to write. Perhaps the greatest and the hardest pleasure that exists. To be autonomous, but to dissolve the self to the service of the reader.

There it is. I read to be selfish. I read because there is nothing else like the pursuit of words to convey ideas and thought and feeling. I have written non-fiction, and I read non-fiction all the time as part of my work. But the books that attract me most, whether fiction or non-fiction, are human stories – people making their lives in the innumerable painful dilemmas that history throws at them. Words that bring ideas and realities that I would not otherwise know, and that I would not imagine without them.

Jordan Peterson
author of *Beyond Order*

The revolutionary technologies of online video and audio – YouTube and podcasts, most particularly – have made it easier to learn by watching and listening, and there is no shortage of high-quality content. Even my advanced university graduate students were often accessing academic information in audio instead of book form. Why read, in the modern world—and, the corollary question, why write? Given that everything can be spoken, and kept perhaps as permanently as the written word; given that there is virtually no barrier to immediate publication and dissemination for video or audio content; given the fact that many more people can watch and listen (and more easily) than can read?

Perhaps we could begin to answer this question by considering not reading, per se (which may be replaceable by audio – more on that in a bit), but writing. What's the difference between writing and speaking spontaneously?

Depth of thought, in a phrase. I have conducted many interviews and discussions, and placed them online, in video and audio form. But I continue to write. Why? Let's consider thought itself for a moment. Perhaps thought can be usefully considered in two forms: revelatory and evaluative. Often, thoughts merely spring to mind. How and why is a mystery. This happens most naturally and immediately in the course of conversation, where the utterance of one participant will give rise to the response of others. And it's not so much that we listen, and think, and then speak in response, but that we speak in response immediately (and that's the thought). I think of that as revelatory because the thoughts, often expressed in speech, make their appearance more or less of their own accord.

Without that, we could not speak, and thought would not exist. But the second component of thought is evaluative, and this is where writing (and, therefore, reading) truly comes into its own. When I am writing something serious, I first ask myself a question, or a series of questions, and wait, in a sense for the answer. That might be regarded as the consequence of a dialogue with myself (or perhaps a group conversation, conducted internally, if I am thinking about something particularly complex). Once the answer – my thought – reveals itself, I try to capture it on paper. But I don't stop there. Once I have written down the thought, affixed it to paper, I can then stand back from it and use the cognitive resources that would otherwise be occupied by questioning or revelation to ask myself another question: Is this thought reliable? Is it well-formulated? Am I willing to stand by it (alternatively: Do I think it is true)? Can I formulate a thought, or more than one thought, in opposition to it, or as an alternative? – and I may write down these new formulations, antitheses and alternatives, and then consider each of them in turn, testing them, arguing with myself, using paper or the electronic equivalent as the forum, and attempting continually to specify a thought, in writing, relying on revelation and evaluation, that I cannot break apart, undermine or supersede.

And that depth of thought – particularly at the evaluative level; the level at which questioning of revelatory thought occurs – is simply not possible in a mere discussion. Thus, for truly serious thought, writing and all the editing that should go along with writing remains absolutely necessary.

The same can be said for reading. While reading, the reader can pause, evaluate the thoughts encountered, sift them, argue internally for or against them, refer back easily to a previous thought, skip ahead easily to see where the argument is going, obtain an overview of the entire work – all, in some sense, difficult to replicate even with the audio version of a written text, an analogue of writing.

This is thought in the truest sense, and the degree to which it truly depends on reading and writing (rather than their analogues, speaking and watching/listening) is unknown. I know what I would miss, however, if I replaced the former entirely with the latter: the possibility of challenging my ability to think at the deepest level.

And that is to say nothing of the pleasure of reading. One day, I was crossing the Harvard campus with my wife, Tammy. We passed the great Harvard library, near the ventilation shaft exhaust. 'Can you smell the books,' I asked Tammy. 'I love the smell of books.' She laughed at my enthusiasm. Just then another professor, a colleague of mine from the psychology department passed by. 'Don't you just love the smell of books,' he said. Both Tammy and I laughed. But it's true, for me. I love books. And there is something real to be said for books as artefacts. I have switched to reading on my phone, through Kindle. I like the ability to take screenshots of pages I want to refer to in my writing. The portability cannot be beaten, and neither can the library/storage function. It is far from obvious to me, however, that I will read as much on my phone as I did when I was relying primarily on books (which I love).

We might consider the retro appeal of vinyl albums in this regard. It is possible to find every song ever recorded, for all intents and purposes, on platforms such as Spotify (which I use intensely). But it's not that easy to find what is new on Spotify. I remember, vividly, from my youth, the excitement that swept the whole culture (or at least that element of the culture interested in music) when a great band was about to release a new album. I remember the appeal of the cover, the brute and glorious fact of the actual physical artefact, the kinship with particularly loved albums that would rapidly develop, the fact that the vinyl disc and its cover itself lent itself to such developments as the concept album.

We know what we gain, we think, when we switch from the physical to the virtual, or from the more difficult (reading and writing) to the easier (listening and talking). But it's not so obvious what we lose.

It would be a great shame to lose reading.

Steven Pinker
author of *Rationality*

The supernova of knowledge continuously redefines what it means to be human. Our understanding of who we are, where we came from, how the world works, and what matters in life depends on partaking of the vast and ever-expanding store of knowledge. To be aware of one's country and its history, of the diversity of customs and beliefs across the globe and through the ages, of the blunders and triumphs of past civilizations, of the microcosms of cells and atoms and the macrocosms of planets and galaxies, of the ethereal reality of number and logic and pattern – such awareness truly lifts us to a higher plane of consciousness. It is a gift of belonging to a brainy species with a long history and the greatest invention of all time, the written word.

The mind-altering effects of literacy extend to every sphere of life, in ways that range from the obvious to the spooky. At the obvious end of the range, a little knowledge about sanitation, nutrition and safe sex can go a long way toward improving health and extending life. Also obvious is that literacy and numeracy are the foundations of modern wealth creation. In the developing world a young woman can't even work as a household servant if she is unable to read a note or count out supplies, and higher rungs of the occupational ladder require ever-increasing abilities to understand technical material. The first countries that made the Great Escape from universal poverty in the nineteenth century, and the countries that have grown the fastest ever since, are the countries that educated their children most intensely.

At the more spiritual end of the range, literacy brings gifts that go well beyond practical know-how and economic growth: better education today makes a country more democratic and peaceful tomorrow. Some of the causal pathways may simply be demographic and economic. Better-educated girls grow up to have fewer babies, and so are less likely to beget youth bulges with their surfeit of troublemaking young men. And better-educated countries are richer, and richer countries tend to be more peaceful and democratic.

But some of the causal pathways implement the highest values of the Enlightenment. So much changes when you get an education! You unlearn dangerous superstitions, such as that leaders rule by divine right, or that people who don't look like you are less than human. You learn that there are other cultures that are as tied to their ways of life as you are to yours, and for no better or worse reason. You learn that charismatic saviours have led their countries to disaster. You learn that your own convictions, no matter how heartfelt or popular, may be mistaken. You learn that there are better and worse ways to live, and that other people and other cultures may know things that you don't. Not least, you learn that there are ways of resolving conflicts without violence. All these epiphanies militate against knuckling under the rule of an autocrat or joining a crusade to subdue and kill your neighbours. Of course, none of this wisdom is guaranteed, particularly when authorities promulgate their own dogmas, alternative facts and conspiracy theories – and, in a backhanded compliment to the power of knowledge, stifle the people and ideas that might discredit them.

Studies of the effects of education confirm that educated people really are more enlightened. They are less racist, sexist, xenophobic, homophobic and authoritarian. They place a higher value on imagination, independence and free speech. They are more likely to vote, volunteer, express political views and belong to civic associations such as unions, political parties and religious and community organizations. They are also likelier to trust their fellow citizens – a prime ingredient of the precious elixir called social capital, which gives people the confidence to contract, invest, and obey the law without fearing that they are chumps who will be shafted by everyone else.

For all these reasons, literacy is an engine of human progress, material, moral, spiritual.

Serhii Plokhy
author of *Nuclear Folly*

Can we really survive these days without reading? The ubiquity of social media, to say nothing of email, does not change but rather underscores this fact: we have to read just to survive in the modern world. Still, there is a difference between reading to keep up with the avalanche of everyday business and reading to ensure our well-being and even survival as a society. We need to make time for reading books – fiction for emotional satisfaction and growth, and non-fiction to make ourselves at home in the world.

To understand the world, to chart our own course and lead others, we have to read non-fiction, and more specifically (here I betray my bias) history. Really good historical works are not just about the past: they are also concerned with the present and the future. They allow us to benefit from the experience of our ancestors and help us identify the challenges of today, calm our nerves, assess our situation realistically, solve current problems by fully comprehending their broader historical context, and plan for the future. The best books of this kind also entertain us, helping us relax and recharge our batteries. The trick is to find them.

Carlo Rovelli
author of *Helgoland*

Why do we breathe? Why do we chat? Why do we look around us?

Because that's what we are, curious critters, thirsty to know, see, learn, discover, enlarge our sight, our vision, our world.

And that's what we find in books: immense spaces of thoughts, ideas, characters, visions, possibilities, perspectives, mental universes that expand what we understand, what we see, what we can do, what we are.

And then, few things are better than sinking into my large round ruby-red couch, with my feet up, soft lighting, letting the world, its worries, its haste, its anguish fade away and transmigrate into the different universe of a story, a poem, an essay, a reflection, or even a manual.

Why *shouldn't* we read? It would be like renouncing seeing friends, walking in the woods, or making love . . .

Priya Satia
author of *Time's Monster*

I

Books are nothing, said the wisemen.

The fifteenth-century mystic poet Kabir addressed priests of his time: *Tu kehta kaagad ki lekhi, main kehta aankhan ke dekhi* (You say what is written on paper; I say what my eyes have seen).

His contemporary Guru Nanak, founder of the future Sikh faith, similarly said: *Parhiye jeti arja parhiye jete saas; Nanak lekhe ik gal hor haume jhakhana jhaakh* (You may spend your whole life in studying, but there is only one thing that matters [His name]; all else is the ego's futile grappling).

The eighteenth-century Sufi poet Bulleh Shah echoed: *Ilmon bas karin o yaar; ikko alif tere darkaar* (Stop this bookish learning, friend; you need just one letter, *alif* [the first letter of 'Allah' and of the Arabic alphabet]).

Three saintly poets asking us to turn our backs on reading – on mere 'bookish' knowledge – in order to grasp true understanding of existence. This was a challenge to the religious power of social elites, since the holy books, the Vedas and the Quran, require knowledge of classical languages that were their monopoly.

Nanak's poems were nevertheless collected in a book, a new holy book accessibly written in the vernacular in the specially developed script of Gurmukhi: the *Guru Granth Sahib*, which also included Kabir's poems. Guru Gobind Singh, who completed the compilation, explained that this was no *mere* book, but the final eternal guru of the Sikh faith.

The book was everything.

This culture – drawing from beyond and spilling beyond Punjab – is one in which we read writing that questions the power of reading.

We read in multiple scripts and divide ourselves based on the scripts we read, while preserving common oral traditions, including religious poetry and the popular *qissas* (epic romances) with which it is entangled. We mistrust books, we bow to books. As Salman Rushdie famously shared with the world: we kiss books.

The printed poems of Bulleh Shah that I read today are not exactly what he composed but what was passed down orally. For a Sufi invested in annihilation of the ego, authorly concern with precise preservation of his poetry made little sense – books were nothing. But I read Bulleh Shah in Gurmukhi, Shahmukhi, and Devanagri, as a mental exercise and practice of dissent, to affirm the syncretism he represents after an era of mass displacements caused by new borders in 1947 and 1966, state violence in the 1980s, and historic patterns of migration. In our Arya Samaji household in Muktsar (site of Guru Gobind Singh's last battle in 1705), my dadi (paternal grandmother) daily read her *gutka*, a small book of Sikh scriptures, in Gurmukhi. She had little if any schooling but read three scripts. I read in three scripts to keep the land of five rivers – '*punj ab*' – intact for me, daughter of a 1947 refugee and 1966 migrant.

Books are everything.

II

Books are nothing, said the mothers.

My refugee nani (maternal grandmother) said that there are many paths to experiencing the divine, but hers was *bhakti*, devotion through worship, rather than *gyan*, knowledge achieved through study. But I saw her, I saw her read incessantly.

Growing up brown in the United States, I found my first white friend in a book in 1978: Ramona Quimby. To know her better, to keep her with me, I began to read with feverish determination. In 1979, I burst upon my mother with the exhilarating news that I had read the entire, boxily thick, chapter-book story of *Ramona and Her Mother* in just two days. She asked, equal measures testy and earnest: 'But what do you get out of reading a storybook?' – surely that mental labour might have been better applied to something *real*, practical.

My mother was raised in a refugee household in a post-colonial place and time: post-1947 Delhi. Why indulge the imagination, when there is work to be done? Problems to be solved. Mouths to be fed. Development. Catch-up. What Frantz Fanon called the 'unending contest' of post-colonial life. Especially from a Punjabi ethical outlook, infused with Bulleh Shah and Sikhism, which sees the world as *real* and our deeds in it as a mode of experiencing the divine.

The suspicion of girls and women reading books, tucked in a corner, in selfish, private enjoyment, exposing themselves to new things and people, new ways: *empowering* themselves. Reading a *gutka* was an acceptably edifying and pacifying form of reading that gave women in a patriarchal world a chance for downtime, mental escape, privacy, at once enabling and subverting that world.

Ramona was a pesky, improper girl, a second daughter (like me), who helped me feel OK in America and in a home awaiting a son. She and countless such friends went with me, everywhere, to the homes of adoptive uncles and aunties in California, to school under my desk, to Muktsar. My most precious possessions, my books.

Books were everything.

I write non-fiction books now. My mother doesn't read them, but she kisses them.

III

Books are everything, said the revolutionaries.

In 1929, when my grandmothers were children, the anti-colonial and socialist revolutionary Bhagat Singh went on hunger strike to demand rights as a political prisoner, including the right to books.

Reading was essential to the 'independent thinking' required of a revolutionary, he explained in an essay written in jail in 1930. Bulleh Shah had turned from books to find God; Bhagat Singh turned to books to lose God, as religious faith, he felt, kept men from recognizing their own ability to act. Anticipating the pedagogical effect of his own writing, he repeatedly addressed his 'readers' as he recounted how reading Marx, Lenin, Trotsky, Darwin, and others had shaped him. But he read non-instrumentally, too: after he was sentenced to death, he continued to demand books, knowing their value would accrue only to him.

His jail diaries brim with notes on that reading. The question 'Why I Read' is inseparable from 'Why I Write', as George Orwell titled a 1946 essay. You write what you know, and what you know is your life, into which your reading has spilled.

The tiny squiggly black lines that create entire worlds for us are intersubjective things, putting us in universal dialogue, communion with all experience. Bulleh Shah valorized experience led by a *murshid* (spiritual guide) over book knowledge. But if a book can be an eternal guru, the distinction blurs. This is why reading fiction and reading non-fiction are not entirely distinct; both have poetic and political functions. Indeed, in the face of planetary crisis, the 'great burden' of 'imaginatively restoring agency and voice to non-humans', a task 'at once aesthetic and political', falls upon storytellers, Amitav Ghosh has said. It is they who can remind us of the collective bonds that other books asked us to forget in an era in which 'a small group of humans [came] to believe that other beings, including the majority of their own species, were incapable of articulation and agency'. They read to subjugate the world.

Bhagat Singh read to catch up with global history, in a colonial world built on the claim that Europe was its fount. For many from formerly colonized, non-white regions, a sense of belatedness still drives voracious reading. While studying at the LSE in the 1990s, I read gluttonously from London's myriad bookshops, determined to join The Culture. To get the Dickens references *and* the Edward Said references. To move in from the margins. It takes time to realize, as

Toni Morrison arrestingly put it, that 'where I already am is the mainstream': this head full of Kabir, Bulleh Shah, Sanskrit shlokas, *and* Ramona, *and* Dickens, *and* Fanon.

We read to escape our own lane. Bhagat Singh read to shake off received wisdom, to question the unjust colonial world he inhabited. In the modern era, the new genre of the novel showcased the idea of highly individuated, internally consistent selfhood, inviting the reader to empathetically connect with this fictional persona. But in this, it, like all fiction (and art more generally), ultimately depended on a brimming, porous sense of self – our capacity to identify with characters and experiences that are entirely other. Humanistic nonfiction, including history, shares this goal and succeeds most when driven by a fundamentally imaginative goal: utopianism, the aspiration for a more just, equitable and loving world. This is its ultimately poetic function and the way it enables practical politics.

That spirit animated Bhagat Singh's writing, and the writing of those he read. Certainly, there are times of cataclysmic breakdown in which we read simply to remain human. More worryingly, there are times, like ours, of such atomization in which we read because we no longer know how to *do* as a collective.

It was oral traditions, along with religious and village practices and union structures, that empowered Punjab's farmers and farmers from across the 1966 borders to uphold the values of collective interdependence in their epic protest of 2020–21. A folkloric Bhagat Singh was among them. After all, real as he was, Singh moulded himself in the first place from the stuff of fiction, drawing from cinema and poetry. Even in his lifetime, his love of homeland was analogized to the love depicted in *qissas* like Heer-Ranjha.

History exceeds the constraints of books and the fiction/nonfiction divide, while we persist in looking for answers by reading – books, Twitter, WhatsApp forwards, the papers – reading everything as we read the backs of cereal boxes, compulsively, helplessly, awaiting the writing that might redeem us, the 'new humanism' Fanon told us we need.

But as we await stories that will allow us to transcend our humanity and reconnect with the non-human and the land, it is worth recalling that that knowledge is already with us, transcendently. It is what Bulleh Shah found in following his *murshid* Shah Inayat, as Heer lost herself in Ranjha. It is the message of the eternal guru, a book.

Books are nothing, but everything.

John Sellars

author of *The Fourfold Remedy*

Francesco Petrarca (Petrarch) was a voracious lover of books. When he was not secluded away in some quiet retreat so that he could read and write, he was out hunting for manuscripts. These were not just any old books but lost works of classical literature, often left abandoned and neglected in a corner of a monastery. His searches took him across Italy, France and Germany. His most celebrated find was a copy of Cicero's letters to his friend Atticus, left unread and forgotten in a library in Verona. These ancient books became so important to Petrarch because, he commented, he did not feel particularly at home in his own time and place – fourteenth-century France and Italy – and so these voices from antiquity were a means of connecting with a different era. That's one reason to read.

On a hiking trip up to the top of Mount Ventoux in southern France, Petrarch took with him a recently acquired copy of Augustine's *Confessions*. Once at the summit he opened the book at a seemingly random page and read the following line: 'men go to marvel at the heights of mountains, the mighty waves of the sea, the wide sweep of rivers, the sound of the ocean, and the movement of the stars, yet they abandon themselves.' These words profoundly shook him. He had been seen. From that point on, he embarked on a journey of introspection and spiritual development. Reading those words of Augustine transformed Petrarch's entire outlook on life. That's a second reason to read.

Petrarch remained a firm admirer of pagan classical literature even after Augustine had spoken to him from the page. He read the letters of Seneca and the philosophical works of Cicero to seek guidance on how to manage his emotions and occasional bouts of depression. He had been grappling with his own emotions throughout his life, especially his love for Laura, the woman who inspired much of his poetry. The ideas and advice of the ancient philosophers helped him to keep his emotions in check. His reading offered him therapy and guidance on how to live a better life. That's another reason to read.

Many of the books that Petrarch read warned against book learning for its own sake. Seneca cautioned about the dangers of reading too much, of jumping from one author to another without taking time to digest what has been said. Petrarch was also critical of the Scholastic teachers of his day, who focused on arguing about ideas in books but failed to learn from them in the way that mattered most, namely extracting lessons in how to live a good life. For Petrarch and the ancient authors who inspired him, reading is not an end in itself. It is a means through which we can be transported to other times and places, be inspired to find out who we are, and gain timeless guidance about how to live.

Emma Smith

author of *This is Shakespeare*

As a child, my greatest treat was to buy a Cadbury's Animal bar – a thin square of pocket-money-sized chocolate bearing the relief image of a giraffe or a lion. I'd open out the foil and break the bar into as many shards as possible. Then I would sit reading my library book in a chair. At each turn of the page, I'd reach out to take a fragment of chocolate. I could make the book, and the chocolate, last for hours of pleasure.

It was decades later, following a beginners' mindfulness guide that involved savouring a square of superior chocolate on the tongue, that I realized that my childhood reading practice was itself a kind of meditation, a training of the mind to the moment. While the library book took me away from my world, the chocolate brought me back to the here and now. The story swept onwards beyond the confines of the printed page; marking each leaf turn with a taste reinstated the materiality, the physicality, of reading as a bodily, not just a cerebral, experience. My reading was an experience of time, as much as it was an experience of content.

The most obvious reason we read is to get away, to escape, to time-travel, to hop into different worlds and consciousnesses and understandings. But I think I have also always read to locate myself more rhythmically within my own environment. Reading is as much a progress through a physical book as it is through a narrative. It is marked by the awareness of the weight of the volume in the hand, the rustle and sensation of its paper, the spring of its spine, the texture of its cover, the wedge of pages yet unread.

I have come to see that reading journey, marked by the regular turning of pages, as a kind of deliberative breathing. The pages of my books are not so much a map of unexplored countries, or a theatre of new possibilities. Rather, they are opened like paired lungs.

A dense printed network of branching bronchial airways takes in and forwards oxygen. Inhaling, exhaling. Verso, recto. It is, literally, all about inspiration.

So, maybe we read rather as we might run, or dance, or undertake mindful breathing, or wear a fitness tracker: to hear our pulse with more attention. That makes reading less the fretful escapology we often seek, and instead, something more fully physically present in the moment. Preferably in a chair, with a library book, accompanied by some splinters of chocolate.

Daniel Susskind
author of *A World Without Work*

Some read non-fiction to 'relax'. I am not sure. For me, it often feels more like a combat sport: grappling with new ideas, sweating over unfamiliar language, tussling with unusual arguments. That said, there is still something more forgiving about non-fiction. Fiction takes no prisoners. It demands that you read the books in full, from cover to cover. But non-fiction tends to let you pick and choose – chapters, sections, paragraphs – and flick through its pages guilt free.

As a writer, I also read to watch others at work: to see how they translate their ideas, boil down complexity, build their stories, set light to dry academic papers. For books on topics close to home, I often imagine myself at the author's desk, fingers on the keyboard, and ask how I might have couched this or explained that. I like to rummage around the footnotes, a writer's attic: full of treasured ideas, not always useful for everyday reading, but ones they simply couldn't let go.

Yet for some, I expect that these sorts of explanation will seem like a rather shallow account of why they read. They will feel it is not simply a means to a narrow end but the source of something much deeper – an identity, rooted in the books they choose to read. The cartoonist Moose Allain captured this spirit in a tweet: 'Your bookshelves are a kind of autobiography.' And he is right. Books shape us, but they also remind us of who we were, the places we read them, the people we were with, and even what we were eating from the stains on the page.

For me, books certainly play that role. In the Qur'an there is a wonderful phrase that is used to describe Jews – the *ahl al-kitab*, or the 'People of the Book'. The book was the Torah, or Hebrew Bible, the sacred text given to Moses by God on Mount Sinai. But today, in our irreligious age, a better term for the many 'secular Jews' like me – those who feel Jewish but do not root that identity in a God – might be the 'People of the Books' instead.

The idea of a 'secular Jew' can puzzle non-Jews and irritate observant Jews. But for me and my fellow-travellers the term nicely captures who we are. Judaism is not only about a Jewish God but a Jewish civilization, about culture rather than faith – shared memories and stories, songs and traditions, ways of living, laughing and eating. And at the core of this identity are books: finding and collecting them, holding and smelling them, arranging (and re-arranging) them – and, of course, reading them.

The role for books in any type of Jewish identity is unsurprising, given the way we are taught to treat them. Drop a Torah scroll, and every Jew present must fast for forty days: an act reserved for moments of atonement or mourning. Don't throw out a tired and faded religious book: it must be buried with proper funeral rights in the ground. Always kiss a prayer book when dropped on the floor and kiss it before returning it to the shelf, never leave a prayer book open if unattended and never build a stack of them with less important ones at the top.

These scattered thoughts are very personal reflections. But I imagine others, from different walks of life, will arrive at a similar conclusion: that non-fiction books matter because we are what we read.

Sofi Thanhauser
author of *Worn*

THE BOOK IS THE LOVER

I discovered a taste for reading American history on a couch up-holstered in blue denim the year my heart was broken for the first time. That heavy yellow textbook resting on my thighs brought the only relief I knew in the spring of my seventeenth year. Because Andrew Jackson and the gold standard and the birth of the railroad: what had they to do with love?

Multitudinous as grass in the field, history's discrete events lay before me, demanding review. Only, unlike grass each stalk was not slim and unitary, but rather held endless, forking branches. There, in that very particular present, under the weight of the yellow book, I felt the air thick with contingency. The Massachusetts that I knew, with its seasonally unemployed commercial fishermen, its Dunkin' Donuts, its lawn topiary so ugly it could cut the soul, its cops who never gave speeding tickets to football players, its menthol cig-arettes, slurpees and gravel pits: all that, along with me and my heartbreak, had been heaved up and spat out by the great engine of history, and there was no denying it. That was assuaging. So was the fact that history was a place where I, personally, had neither sinned nor erred. I hadn't damaged it and couldn't. Nothing is more calm-ing than the conflicts of the long-since dead.

Absorption in the nineteenth century was an anesthetic at the moment that I felt love's disappointment. But eventually I came to consider that reading is not a mere consolation prize for losers in the game of desire, it is something weirder. The book, I concluded, is the original lover. After all, long before the human lover arrives, the *book* is the other body in the bed. The hand caresses it. Observe a person's mouth while reading: slack, vegetal, languid as a flower.

Observe a person's eyes while reading: dulcet, sensual. If they are not a lover's eyes they are the eyes of a baby at the breast, pupils sliding along smugly. Those are the same eyes.

Young people believe the book to be the lover's interlocutor and not the lover proper. Like many young people, I read books in anticipation of someday meeting the someone who had read them also. I imagined our communion, how the two of us would recall together the grim flavour of Grushenka as she steps out from behind the curtain. It is less strange to imagine it that way than to acknowledge what has happened already: that one is really in love with the dead. That the dead Dostoyevsky knows more of the soul than the living friend.

The book, that mute reflection of the warmth and the pulsations and the tiresome longings of the self, has no heartbeat, that is true. A paradox: one needs a body to read, but in reading one imagines independence from that very body, and even from the tightrope of the mind, its angry clanging. Two lovers, one bodiless, another for whom that body is irrelevant.

I once asked a poet, 'Do you think we are all actually the same person?' and she said, 'No.' If *that*'s true, is it because we all have separate bodies? And if that's true, is it true after bodies end? Or is there still a little particular heat left behind in the book after the body of the writer is gone? Do the words of the dead separate out from her like a dry husk, or is there juice or meat left in the claw? Dryness is not final. Some books lie like dried up stream beds until seasonal floods fill them. The phase of the moon, the quantity of rain, the volume of water taken up by crops upstream: all those might dictate when a river runs full again, or a book breathes with meaning again, along with the voice, or the moan, of the woman who made it: her blood, her bone, her meat. And if, as I had learned while reading history with a broken heart, the present world must have somehow slipped and spat its way out of the womb of that other one, the one filled with the dead, surely some of those books were our mothers, also.

Shashi Tharoor

author of *Inglorious Empire*

I grew up as an asthmatic child in an India without television, and I was often too ill to simply go out and play with friends. Personal computers, mobile phones and Play Station hadn't been dreamed of, so, sitting propped up in bed, struggling to breathe, there was only one option for me: I read.

I read everything I could lay my hands on, from the books on my parents' shelves to the copies of *Reader's Digest* that my father subscribed to and mercifully never threw away. Reading was my escape, my entertainment, my education.

My asthma got better with time as new medicines were invented, but the reading habit proved as chronic an affliction. At school and college, I read well beyond the textbooks required by the syllabus. As an impecunious graduate student in the United States, skipping meals to make ends meet on my scholarship, I found my spare-time diversion in reading books, in preference to alternative forms of entertainment I couldn't afford. So, when I started my working life and actually could afford to splurge on recreational pleasures, it was in bookshops that I did so. Reading was a habit: I had become conditioned to be a reader.

As my working life got busier and the hours longer, and with ever more distractions available for the weary, the time for reading shrank. Today the ubiquitous screens around me – television, desktop computer, laptop, tablet, mobile phone – keep demanding my time, and I find I need to make more and more of an effort to simply open a book.

Reading seems to demand more, and offer less, than any of those screens. Books require attention, concentration, patience, the possession of a vocabulary and the talent to conjure worlds out of patterns of black-and-white ink on the page. Screens give you visual images, assault your senses, flesh out what books can only describe, leave little to the imagination and require hardly any work from you to absorb. And they respond to the time-pressures of the busy working adult. A novel that might take you eight or nine hours to read over several days can be reduced to its essence and enacted for you on the screen in less than two.

And yet – I read. I read because I thrill to the process of discovery that the printed word allows but visual media simplifies. I revel in the level of detail that reading gives me but the screen abridges. I enjoy being challenged to interpret what I read and to apply my own mind to imagining the world the author is depicting, rather than allowing a film-producer to imagine it for me.

In a world of fast food, bullet trains and T-20 cricket, I find greater meaning in the slow read. The process of engaging with the printed word requires more effort, but I would rather make that effort than remain the passive recipient of someone else's imagination.

Books are like the toddy-tapper's hatchet, cutting through the rough husk that enshrouds our minds to the exhilaration that ferments within. More than a century ago, Walter Pater wrote of art as 'professing frankly to give nothing but the highest quality to your moments as they pass'. That may be all that reading offers; but it is no modest aspiration.

Gaia Vince

author of *Transcendence*

I read to mind-travel. To be transported to another place and time. Sometimes the writer joins me; sometimes I'm given other companions. For as long as I am immersed in story, I am emotionally connected to the writer's world as if I were experiencing it outside of my imagination. Reading is a reprieve from reality, from the increasing demands of life off the page, but it is not a disengagement from feelings, from empathy, from caring.

It starts with story. Stories are a hugely important human survival tool that have shaped our societies, our understanding of the world and relationship to our environment, and even our biology – our brains have evolved to understand the world through narrative, making stories phenomenally powerful cultural tools. Storytelling is an inherently social enterprise – it relies on people sharing a mental commons, agreeing together to suspend reality and explore a virtual space-time. Stories make our societies more cooperative and help us cooperate as individuals. We pass around information about ourselves and our world through stories, learning how to behave and how to empathize. Through stories we can explore the human condition and see how other people think.

People who spin narratives for a living are celebrated throughout the world. The Agta, a Filipino hunter-gatherer population, value storytelling more than any other skill – twice as much as hunting ability – and the best storytellers have the most children, anthropologists report.

It was through reading that I discovered that my deepest, most traumatic pain, like my private passions – so exhilarating but confusing – were not, after all, unique to me. That I was not the first person in the world to experience bloodcurdling embarrassment or crushing heartbreak or the anguish of unrequited love. Not only was

I not alone in this, but I had fellow soulmates, brothers and sisters in arms, going back thousands of years, who could speak to me, sitting in my late-twentieth-century bedroom, about our shared experiences.

I read to learn. Through imagined accounts, sure, but, more significantly, through the written experiences of others and the deeply researched learnings of writers building on other writers – the cumulative cultural evolution of our species made visible in the stacks of bound print on processed trees that line the walls of our buildings. I read to understand the most pressing issues on my mind, the crises of our time – climate change, biodiversity loss, cultural and social devastation. I read as a line fisher, dangling my hook in a vast body of literature, hoping to hook some nuggets, hoping to learn where in this huge ocean of knowledge are the enticing shoals I seek. Then I read like a free-diver, hunting across the expert reefs of the most pertinent research publications, looking for pearls. I sift and sort my learnings, and to them I add my own, continuing the creative process that nourishes this cultural ecosystem.

I read so I can write. I write so others can read, to continue the conversation that began five millennia ago and will continue far into the future. Books are immortal, writings live on, re-enlivened with every new interpretation. Books explain the world and teach us how to respond to it as solo navigators and collectively as a society. I write to add myself to the record. To produce versions, however sophisticated, of 'I woz ere!' A sort of literary tagging across the media landscape of my short time on this 4.6-billion-year-old planet. I write to convey something new from my time and place, to dissect the complex and secretive world of science and translate it, open it up to non-specialists.

How amazing it is that with twenty-six letters encoded in our inherited language we can describe the ideas in our heads to another mind. We can invent creatures not feasible but believable, scenarios of the past and future, and make ourselves understood to strangers, set them laughing or crying, mind talking to mind. Writing preserves those thoughts, that language, those exact sentences. But it does more than that: it creates them, too. When we speak, our words dissolve in the instant of their utterance, in the moment of their being heard, like a cloud of warm breath disappearing into cold air. We can be vague or clumsy, inarticulate or imprecise. As fast as our speech dissolves, we fill the space with new words, occupying the listener's opportunity for interrogation with the business of listening. There is no re-reading, re-examining with heard speech. Words flow, off-the-cuff in-accuracies excused in the trade for immediate delivery, passionate personalization.

Writing is different. When you commit words to paper you make them permanent, you must make a decision about the choice of words and their order, the sentences you craft, and the subjects you name. Text is from the Latin *texere*, to weave, because we weave our words just as we weave textiles. An argument can be built transpar-ently and, however robust, is exposed to consideration and attack. Learning to read and write, like most culturally acquired skills, changes our biology. Literate people have different brains from illit-erate people by around age eight, because their visual processing systems have been specialized for reading (often at the expense of, say, facial recognition). Highly literate people become word spotters in the same way that a hunter-gatherer is able to detect the nuances that reveal animal tracks. Our eyes jump to word patterns in our native script, and we unconsciously decipher them, compulsively reading across our environment. This ability to explore the world through reading occurs far earlier than our physical freedom. By the time my children reached four years old, they had enough reading ability to independently discover and source information – mind experiences – that I hadn't introduced them to. They were, for the first time, learning about the world through their own volition and out of my careful control.

Reading and writing are solitary tasks but, for me, essential. I don't have tolerant enough friends with whom it would be possible or appropriate to have the kinds of conversation I have on the page. The library holds those friends for me. Thousands upon thousands of conversations from all manner of perspectives – and some to which I will also contribute.

Esmé Weijun Wang

author of *The Collected Schizophrenias*

I have found that one of life's greatest fundamental frustrations – as well as one of its greatest terrors – is that I have only one life, and that every choice I make is finite. I have made certain decisions that have led me down certain alleys, and whether I am happy or not with the route I am on is not so much the point; the point is that I did not choose any of the centillion other paths that I could have gone down. I did not choose to research octopuses or become a carpenter or live in Taipei. A well-known researcher told me, while I was attempting to decide my next moves, that the field of social psychology would be poorer if I did not pursue it. Well: I didn't become a social psychologist, and I don't know what would have happened if I did.

Reading non-fiction is one way that I can access these unselected avenues. I can choose to learn about the soul of an octopus, or the ins and outs of building a table. I never became a social psychologist, but the library of books written by such people is so vast that I could spend the rest of my life reading only those books, and I still wouldn't be able to read more than a fraction.

In my one life, I have experienced chronic illness, disability and psychosis. In reading the memoirs of others, I see that I am not alone. I become part of a community of fellow travellers, and their words allow me to consider alternatives that I could not have chosen or stumbled into. What if I had been born in a different country, or existed in a different era? What might I have learned from those wildly foreign experiences? In my worst bouts of despair, I return again and again to Victor Frankl's *Man's Search for Meaning*. I did not live his life – and there but for the grace of God go I – but I am able to learn how to endure my own suffering by reading about how he endured his in a concentration camp during the Holocaust.

I read because I have only one life, and one path to pick my way along. I am lucky enough to see the roads taken and landscapes inhabited by the writers of other books, and, it seems, people have seen the fields of my travails through mine. I hope that I can spend the rest of my days writing and reading and, by doing so, exploring the vastness of existence.

Ralf Webb

author of *Rotten Days in Late Summer*

What's a reasonable number of books to bring with you on, say, a weekend trip? One or two? Three? Ten? I usually go for the latter: that is, more than I could possibly read. I imagine various unlikely situations or crises from which these books, their company, might rescue me. What if I can't sleep; what if I experience an incapacitating homesickness or loneliness; what if I miss a connection and end up stranded overnight at a train station in the middle of nowhere? (At the very least, a couple of paperbacks could serve as a half-decent pillow, in a fix.) Even at eighteen, in Paris for the first time, I found myself alone in the January snow and realized I'd brought at least a dozen books with me, but forgot to pack a winter coat ...

This is not a point of pride: I mean it to sound exactly as obsessive and *excessive* as it is. Yet I still compulsively pack too many books, even if it's only to cross the river and back on the overground. In my rucksack, currently: John Cheever's *Journals* (well-thumbed), David Berman's *Actual Air* (borrowed from a friend, never returned), Janet Malcolm's *Iphigenia in Forest Hills* (bought four years ago, still unread).

Wherever this weird, preposterous faith in the salvationist powers of books comes from, it's a faith that's shared by many writers. Cheever, in those *Journals*: 'Literature has been the salvation of the damned; literature, literature has inspired and guided lovers, routed despair ...'

All of us who hold to it – or at least once held to it – have, I think, experienced something similar in our reading lives, something that got us hooked. We've felt that irreplaceable, inarticulable *click*, the uncanny feeling that a writer – a poet, novelist, playwright, memoirist, journalist, whoever – is speaking across decades, centuries or even millennia, and, stranger still, that they are speaking specifically to ... *us*. Light seems to break through fog – fog that you hadn't even realized was *there* – to illuminate the Chosen Reader. It's not a sensation of having your own thoughts or experiences parroted back to you (there are plenty of other media designed for that purpose). This particular *click* is the very opposite of alienation, exclusion, disconnection: it is, in fact, a kind of communion.

Poetry was the first genre in which I found such moments in abundance. From Frank O'Hara's *Meditations in an Emergency*, one of the dozen books I stuffed in my bag for Paris, or Anne Carson's *Autobiography of Red*, which I once carried around with me everywhere I went for months on end.

At times, this faith in books can be more like an affliction. If you're anything like me, you'll have spent a lot of time reading a great many books *in pursuit* of that experience of communion ... but you'll only rarely rediscover it. Friends might grab you by the shoulders and claim they've found it, thrusting a book into your hands, promising that it will 'change your life' – and you might be disappointed to find that it just doesn't. Worse, you might lend someone a book that speaks to you, only for it to be met with *their* dead-eyed indifference. But that's OK. It's different for everyone. Luckily, there's no shortage of books.

Of course, there are other reasons why we read: to educate and entertain, to complicate and clarify and to provoke discussion. But – for me, anyway – at the bedrock is the faith that it is possible to pull from the chaos and disorder and utter arbitrariness of the world some missive, some scrap of a phrase, some moment of timeless, knife-like insight that enlarges your spirit and brings you into a strange and fleeting synthesis – even if you do happen to find yourself alone in the snow, temporarily without a coat.

David Wengrow

co-author of *The Dawn of Everything*

ON DEEP READING AND HUMAN HISTORY

> Cang Jie, the scribal officer of the Yellow Emperor
> (Huangdi), saw the tracks of the hooves and claws of
> birds and beasts, and knowing that he could divide
> them by type and thus differentiate them, he for the first
> time invented writing and inscribing.
>
> *– From the* Shuo wen jie zi, AD 120

Neuroscientists have come up with a remarkable discovery: our
brains are hard-wired for reading.

On the face of it, this makes no sense. Archaeologists (like me)
believe the human species has existed, with brains and bodies essentially like ours, for over 200,000 years. But the earliest evidence for
writing and reading goes back no further than ancient Egypt and
Mesopotamia, a little more than 5000 years ago, and literacy rates
were low. Alphabets came later still. Yet, today, neurotypical humans
all over the world share an innate capacity for reading. At speeds that
zip by our conscious minds, the human gaze scans written characters
on a page and processes them into sounds, words, and meanings (just
as yours is doing now).

So, the puzzle is this. A few thousand years is just a blink of the
eye, in evolutionary terms. How, over such a short time, did our
minds acquire an innate capacity to respond to written signs in such
ways, especially when so few members of our species were literate
to begin with? There is another way to pose the problem, which
seems just as intractable. How is it that, at some much more remote
point in our evolutionary past, the human brain became attuned to
a technology that did not yet even exist?

In fact, it didn't quite happen in either of those ways. What cognitive scientists find is that reading is an extension of more elementary processes of shape recognition: not just any shapes, but a specific inventory of line combinations and junctures (much as the author of *Shuo wen jie zi*, China's oldest extant dictionary, imagined). Throughout history, scripts that have been widely adopted – from ancient Mesopotamian cuneiform and Scandinavian runes, to modern standard Arabic and Latin – can be seen to conform to, and exploit, these innate processing mechanisms. We also now know that those mechanisms reside in a particular region of the brain, the 'visual word form area', which our species acquired deep in its evolutionary past, long before we invented writing.

What do these evolutionary findings mean for those who love to read?

On the one hand, they confirm that we are wired for reading, and help to explain the otherwise bewildering fact that our children often have to unlearn the ability to read and write in both directions (a capacity that the ancient Greeks, by contrast, chose to exploit, calling it *boustrophēdón* - writing 'as the ox turns', while ploughing). On the other, they account for one of the most common and distressing facts of modern life: most of the time, we don't really read. Our eyes scan the printed matter on the page or the shapes on the screen. Our brains fire up, rendering the images into words at lightning speeds, with little conscious effort on our part. But because it all comes so easily to most of us, we can effectively read without reading; that is, without actually engaging in the kind of deep thought processes that we tend to associate with the *idea* of reading.

Basically, we are too good at reading for our own good, and our digital technologies exploit the innate capacity to read like never before. We read in gasps, squeezed on to crowded train platforms, navigating between apps and devices. Arguably, we read more than ever, but we seem to 'read' less and less as a form of deep engagement with another mind: the mind of a writer. Might we then wonder not 'why we read' but 'how we read'?

Reading a book, for example, is a physical, not just a cognitive, act. But it is a strange one, which puts the rest of the body in suspended animation, so the mind can roam free over the page. Of course, there are many other styles of reading, less static or isolated. We find them in world religions, for example, where reading is often less solitary and more of a social performance: a rhythm with a shared beat, played out in architectural spaces made for that purpose. Do we want deep reading to be a part of our species' future? Can we find the repose to let our thoughts linger again over written words? If so, then there may be a clue here about what this might involve.

Perhaps the answer lies in our ability to rediscover reading as a special kind of social activity, even, perhaps, a slightly sacred one.

Lea Ypi
author of *Free*

I did not choose to start reading books – I was more or less forced to. I have no memories of learning to read or of declaring my appreciation for stories. I only remember that, as a child, the sentence 'read a book' was the answer I was likely to receive in response to the sentence 'I'm bored'. The suggestion came in a tone that made it clear I had no choice but to comply: half way between an offer and a threat.

The fact that reading never began as a free choice, that it was initially an activity more or less inflicted on me, meant that books could never be fully separated from anger: the anger I felt about the circumstances in which I was forced to experience reading and my powerlessness to change them. But I also discovered, early on, that books can help you articulate your anger. They give you a kind of freedom in unfreedom; they enable, if not quite the overcoming of anger, a form of understanding that helps you come to terms with it. I could travel to different places while staying in my room, meet different people while only talking to myself, project myself into different times while remaining firmly rooted in the present. Books helped me let my anger be, devise strategies of rebellion, and find imaginary companions in my struggles. This may also explain why the books I was first attracted to – mainly children's adaptations of Homer and classical Greek myths – were full of angry characters. Achilles' wrath was especially comforting: it was a great solace to discover that even gods and superheroes could feel as powerless as I did.

I never chose to read: the choice was made for me. But that is perhaps how we are all thrust into a culture, of which books form the most important part. We hardly select to be part of that culture: we are born into it, no matter what we do. If we are not readers, we will be literary characters, subjects of historical study, objects of scientific experimentation or social protagonists of the many efforts to understand the world. And since we are all part of a culture in this neither purely voluntary nor purely coercive way, that very dilemma is likely to cause the same discomfort, even anger, that I experienced as a child. We can choose to remain angry, disengaged, lonely, bored, or all of these at once, or we can find ways of relating to others by sharing the discomforts we experience and identifying ways of responding to them. In other words, we can produce and absorb knowledge by being more conscious of the ways in which the production of culture is a collective, trans-generational effort, where the first step to playing a more effective role is becoming aware of our relationship to it.

Reading is one of the few activities we engage with that is both completely solitary and thoroughly collective. 'When evening comes,' Machiavelli wrote in a famous letter to Francesco Vettori, 'I return to my house and enter my study; and at the door I take off the day's clothing, covered with mud and dust, and put on garments regal and courtly; and reclothed appropriately, I enter the ancient courts of ancient men, where, received by them with affection, I feed on the food which only is mine and which I was born for, where I am not ashamed to speak with them and to ask them the reason for their actions; and they in their humanity reply to me.'

Reading is both instrumental – we read to find out more or to challenge what we think we know – and expressive. It is a search for truth that takes place in the awareness that everything we find is fragmentary, partial, located in a specific time and place, controlled by a few, shaped by trends, made to serve particular – often troublesome – ends. But, in the experience of searching for authenticity in the midst of alienation, we also discover humanity in its most hopeful form: this desperate yet relentless effort of meaning-making.

'I feel no boredom. I forget every pain, I do not fear poverty, death does not frighten me,' Machiavelli continues. Books embody a search for agency through which we try to appropriate a world that we do not make from scratch but discover with flaws, and to which we respond by understanding it, challenging what we know, trying to change what we do. When we read, we encounter not this or that person but humanity as such, or rather an ideal of human relations where the urge to speak and the will to be understood are the simple, universal tools through which to express particularity and overcome exclusion.

And in this cross-spatial, cross-temporal, collective effort through which we together appropriate a shared world and create a culture that belongs to all, we catch a glimpse of social freedom.

Slavoj Žižek

author of *Like a Thief in Broad Daylight*

I AM NOT MIKHAIL SUSLOV

Why – or, rather, how – do I read? I practise a violent reading, a reading which tears (what appear as) organic unities apart and takes them out of their context, establishing new unexpected links between fragments. These links do not operate at the level of continuous linear historical progress: they rather emerge at points of 'dialectics at a standstill' (Walter Benjamin), in which a present moment, in a kind of transhistorical short-circuit, directly echoes homologous moments in the past.

Such a reading breaks out of the space of the standard opposition between the immanent reading, which tries to remain faithful to the interpreted text, and the practice of quotation, which uses fragments of a text to justify present ideological and political measures. The exemplary case of such practice is found in Stalinism: the key to Leninism as (Stalinist) ideology is provided by Mikhail Suslov, the member of the Politburo responsible for ideology from Stalin's late years to the time of Brezhnev. Neither Khrushchev nor Brezhnev would release any document until Suslov had looked over it – why? Suslov had an enormous library of Lenin's quotes in his Kremlin office; they were written on index cards, organized by themes and contained in wooden filing cabinets. Every time a new political campaign, economic measure or international policy was introduced, Suslov found an appropriate quote from Lenin to support it. Lenin's quotes in Suslov's collection were isolated from their original contexts. Because Lenin was an extremely prolific writer who commented on all sorts of historical situations and political developments, Suslov could find appropriate quotes to legitimate as 'Leninist' almost any argument and initiative, sometimes even if they opposed each other: 'the very same quotes from the founders of

Marxism-Leninism that Suslov successfully used under Stalin and for which Stalin so highly valued him, Suslov later employed to critique Stalin.' This was the truth of Soviet Leninism: Lenin served as the ultimate reference, and a quote of his legitimized any political, economic or cultural measure, but in a totally pragmatic and arbitrary way – in exactly the same way, incidentally, that the Catholic Church refers to the Bible. The irony is thus that the two big orientations of Marxism – the Stalinist one and the authentic one – can be perfectly grasped through two different modes of quotation.

What Benjamin conceptualized and practised (together with Hegel, Marx, Lenin, Brecht, Jameson and many others) was a radically different practice of quotation, quotation as a form of struggle with the quoted text as well as with the writer's own predicament. Materialist quotation is internal to the quoted original through its very externality to it: its violent disfiguration of the original is in some sense more faithful to the original than the original itself, since it echoes social struggles that traverse both. In his wonderful *How to Talk about Books You Haven't Read*, Pierre Bayard demonstrates (in an ironic reasoning which is ultimately meant quite seriously) that, in order to really formulate the fundamental insight or achievement of a book, it is generally better *not* to read it all – too much data only blurs our clear perception. For example, many essays on Joyce's *Ulysses* – often the best ones – were written by scholars who did not read the whole book; the same goes for books on Kant or Hegel, where a truly detailed knowledge can only give rise to a boring specialist's exegesis, not to living insights. The best interpretations of Hegel are always partial: they extrapolate the totality from a particular figure of thought or of dialectical movement. As a rule, it is not a direct reading of a thick book of Hegel himself but some striking detailed observation – often wrong or at least one-sided – made by an interpreter that allows us to grasp Hegel's thought in its living movement. Hegel's basic lesson is thus the exact opposite of the standard notion of 'totality', which enjoins us to locate a thing into the infinitely complex network of its relations and interdependences: dialectical progress occurs through abstraction, through violent reduction.